Fathers Speak © 2018 Emily R. Long

Printed in the United States of America

First Printing 2018

ISBN: 978-0-9965556-8-5

Firefly Grace Publishing
Burlington, VT 05403

www.EmilyRLong.com

Interior and Cover Design: ShiftFWD

FATHERS SPEAK:

On the Death of a Child

In memory of Ryan

Honoring the father you never got to be to the daughter you
never got to know.

You would have been an amazing dad.

For all the fathers of loss,
too often unseen and unacknowledged.

We honor you and your amazing father love.

FOR THE DADS

Dear Fathers,

This book is for you. It is written by fathers of loss for fathers of loss. It has been my honor to collect these stories from fathers from around the world. These fathers took the time and energy and, let's face it, real emotional labor to share their stories and contribute to this book. In doing so, they offer their words, their support, and their understanding to other fathers like you – fathers grieving and missing their precious children.

It has been apparent to me the lack of resources and support specifically for fathers of loss. Too often it seems that all the focus, attention, and care is directed toward mothers of loss and that fathers can be forgotten and disregarded. You deserve more. You deserve to be seen and heard through this most unbearable loss.

I hope this books helps you to know that you are not forgotten. A father's love is an irreplaceable gift and your children have been blessed with this gift. You deserve all the support, care, and love in the world as you learn to live with this loss.

My hope is that this book can offer some of that support and care and love – even if only in a small way. I hope that it can help bring fathers together to lean on each other and to support each other in a way that feels nurturing and beneficial and comforting.

Most of all, I want you to know that you are not alone. If you feel forgotten, if you feel lost, if you feel alone – I hope that this book will bring you a sense of acknowledgement, recognition, and not-alone-ness.

You are an amazing father. Your children are so very lucky to have you as their dad.

xoxo,
Emily

MATHILDA

Oh You Brave, Brave Father,

From the bottom of my heart, I want you to know that you are not alone. While there are so few people in the world who can truly understand your devastation, I do. We do, and we are here for you. In the days, weeks, months, and years to come, you may hear some say, "Don't worry. You'll have another baby." I know they don't understand. They can't. For them, it is impossible to comprehend the crippling scope of all that you've lost.

You lost the comfort of coming home to your cooing baby and her glowing mother. You lost the weight of her in your arms. You lost the joy of watching his first steps and the thrill of his first words. You lost lullabies and bedtime stories. You lost play dates and playgrounds. You lost temper tantrums, tender moments, and sweet little toes. You lost first days of school and summer vacations. You lost tee ball games and field trips and parent-teacher conferences. You lost first dates, birthdays, holidays, and graduations. You lost their incredible talent, their fiery spirit, their brilliant mind, their sensitive heart. You lost your hopes and dreams for who your precious baby could become. You lost your role as teacher, caretaker, provider, and protector. You lost a part of yourself. You lost your future.

In March of 2016, we lost our sweet daughter, Mathilda, shortly before her birth at 40 weeks and 4 days. For me, every day remains a labyrinth of worry and wonder and where to go next. These are endless empty days, all full of quiet and stillness where there should be a cacophony and constant motion. I am perpetually engulfed by the burning awareness of how different my life should be. To think that I could have anything of value to offer you feels arrogant and heavy. However, there are some things I've been told that I think you should know.

You are a father. More than that, you are the strongest and most courageous kind of father. You love and nurture a baby you can never hold.

You did nothing wrong. This is not your fault. There is nothing you could have done to save your child.

Your grief is normal. If you have a hat your baby wore and you want to kiss it goodnight, do it. If you want to stare in the sky and tell them about your day, go for it. Read them stories. Preserve their nursery. Plant flowers and build a birdhouse for them. Honor them in any way that fills your soul. Nobody can tell you how to parent your dead child. Nobody can judge your grief.

Be patient with yourself and your baby's mother. There is no timetable for grief. There is no getting over so devastating a loss. All you can do is learn to live with it. Like any weight, it may get lighter the longer you lift it, but it will always be yours to carry.

My darling Mathilda was arrestingly beautiful, just like her mother. She had her mom's hands, but she had my skin. She had my hair, but she had her mom's nose. She was our sweet Peanut, our first daughter and our only child. The days and months since we lost her have been the darkest of my life. The only light that I've found has been in the belief that she is the energy that drives all of the wonder in the world. She is the sun that warms my skin and she's the snow in my hair. She's the waves that crash, the breeze that cools, and the rains that bring life. She's the leaves that fall and she's the sand between my toes. She is every bird song, every butterfly, and every rainbow. She fills my world with all of the beauty she can muster, and I find her in that. I find her everywhere I can.

You are an intrepid father, loyal and true. In time, I hope that you can find some of what you lost.

In hope and solidarity,

Jonathan Saulmon

Mathilda's Daddy
Born Still on March 4th, 2016
www.lostlullabies.weebly.com

Previously published in "From Father to Father: Letters from Loss Dad to Loss Dad"

The only light that I've found has been in the belief that she is the energy that drives all of the wonder in the world. She is the sun that warms my skin and she's the snow in my hair. She's the waves that crash, the breeze that cools, and the rains that bring life. She's the leaves that fall and she's the sand between my toes. She is every bird song, every butterfly, and every rainbow. She fills my world with all of the beauty she can muster, and I find her in that. I find her everywhere I can.

HANNAH RAE

I remember the day I held my beautiful daughter in my arms. The joy I felt was remarkable as her eyes gazed back into mine. She was perfect, everything about her was absolutely perfect. If you were to tell me then that I would never be able to hold her in my arms again, I would not have believed you. Looking back, I wish someone would have given me a warning. I would have told her so much. I would have never put her down. I would have done everything I possibly could to save her from that fate, but I had no warning. Just like that, my life was turned upside down.

The guilt and heaviness upon my heart often felt like an anchor. A father's job is to ensure safety and provide for his family. I had felt as if I failed beyond retribution. She was dependent on me since her conception into this world, yet I failed her. I knew deep inside she did not blame me, but I could not seem to dismiss the point that I could not protect her. I had to get it off my mind, off my heart. I wrote her my apologies and told her how much I loved her, missed her, and the fact that I would cherish her forever. I wrote this all to her in the form of a poem, one which I read aloud at her memorial, one which is buried with her, one which had to be written to clear my own mind.

Perhaps the most immediate, disturbing, and vivid reaction to her loss was the infinite amount of questions soaring through my mind. "How did you let this happen?" "Was there anything I could do?" "Did I not pray hard enough?" "Am I being punished?" "Could God have saved her if he wanted to?" "If God loved me would he let this happen?" "Why?" These and many more argued amongst each other vigorously in my head to the point I was mentally exhausted. I found the only way to free my mind was to exclaim, "Be still and leave me alone!" Instantaneously the thoughts ceased and I was left with the question, "Why?" I have still yet to know the answer to that question. I have come to realize and am able to accept that I may never know the answer, and that is ok. Knowing the "why" will not reverse the tragedy that occurred. Knowing the "why" will not heal the pain or offer a substitute. Knowing the "why" could create an even greater amount of grief and sorrow.

The days to follow that treacherous night were frantic. At first it seemed like a horrible nightmare. Is she really gone? Was she really here? It all seemed so confusing and unreal;

however, my wife's tears assured me I had not dreamt it at all. Words cannot describe the feelings and emotions experienced by a parent as they hold their living child for what they know to be the very last time. That specific hour continues to haunt me to this day. "There is nothing else we can do for her. Let us know when you are ready." I did not want to accept the doctor's words as truth. I did not want to let go. I was not ready to let go. I don't recall how much time passed as I continued to stare at my beautiful child, but it was enough time for me to realize that a father is never ready to let go of their child. However, I knew I had to do what was best for my daughter at that moment. Therefore, I lied and said, "I'm ready." In no way or form was I ever ready or prepared for the days to come with her absent from my side.

The unsuspecting call from the hospital the next day was just one example of how unprepared my wife and I were. "Who will be picking up the body?" they had asked. We had no idea how this worked. There is no "Preparing for your Child's Death for Dummies" reference book to educate one on the next steps. Ignorant to the process, we found ourselves driving around to funeral homes repeating each time that our child passed away less than 24 hours ago and we have no idea what to do now. Some appeared sympathetic, while others displayed no symptoms of empathy at all. What they did share in common was their attempts to make the consumer feel they were there to help them through this tragedy while soliciting the many costs of their services. Finally, we had found one person who seemed to truly sympathize for our situation. He took the time to walk us through the legal necessities, while at the same time asking us what we wanted the funeral to be like. In the end, he waived many of the costs associated with his services and arranged everything exactly as we asked. I look back and am thankful we had his assistance and can only imagine what the end result would have been with a different provider.

Over the next few weeks, family and friends kept silent as best they could. They soon found themselves at a loss for words, which was not surprising. The pain associated with the loss of a child is so unique, so unnatural, so unbearable. Many parents never do and never should have to experience that pain. I unfortunately was one of the unlucky ones. Rather than words of sympathy, acts of kindness and love were bestowed upon my wife and I in the weeks to come. My father and brother came to mow the yard while friends and neighbors ensured we did not have to cook for many weeks ahead by taking turns delivering fresh, homemade meals. An online fundraiser and a bake sale were coordinated to relieve some of the unexpected, financial burden associated with the loss of a loved one (and that burden can be heavy). We were blessed to have such wonderful family and friends rush to our aid as soon as they had heard the devastating news. Without a doubt, the lack of their support would have made this journey much more difficult.

Months go by as the showers of blessings and support eventually turn to droplets. I began to feel an expectation from those around me to return to the normalcy of what my life was, as if I was supposed to shrug my shoulders, put the memories of that fateful day in a box, and place it high upon the shelf. The tragedy which I relived daily in my own mind was simply replaced by "the next big thing" in their own. It is not their fault. They simply cannot understand the intensity and grasp that the loss of a child could play upon one's feelings and emotions. The awkward exchange of silence between co-workers eventually graduated to a casual greeting or insensitive story of how wonderful their life is going or the sharing of their children's pictures to show that their child is growing up so quickly. Rather than feeling joy and excitement for them, I found myself unconsciously and uncontrollably placing judgment and resentment upon them. I knew I could not fault them for wanting to express their joy with their current situation, but that everlasting store for them. From the heart and mind of one grieving soul to another...don't give up, His plan for you is not finished. Though your life may feel shattered now, it is just beginning! When you awake in the morning and you see that pink sunrise, or whatever it is that triggers your emotions, smile and know that they love you.

Andrew Borden

"There is nothing else we can do for her. Let us know when you are ready." I did not want to accept the doctor's words as truth. I did not want to let go. I was not ready to let go. I don't recall how much time passed as I continued to stare at my beautiful child, but it was enough time for me to realize that a father is never ready to let go of their child. However, I knew I had to do what was best for my daughter at that moment. Therefore, I lied and said, "I'm ready." In no way or form was I ever ready or prepared for the days to come with her absent from my side.

NOAH

A message to our family and friends:

"Our son, Noah Thomas Purcell, was born at 10.36am on 17th April 2016 in the Royal Brisbane Woman's Hospital Birth Suite after an intense 12 hour labour. Eryn was induced due to developing mild pre-eclampsia symptoms quickly over the weekend, and while this didn't seem to affect Noah to begin with, the last hour of labour saw him in a large amount of distress. When he was born he did not breathe and his heart rate was very low. The wonderful team of doctors and midwives did their absolute best and managed to stabilise his heartbeat, but he unfortunately could not breathe on his own.

The diagnosis for our little monkey was not good. Survival was questionable, with severe brain damage apparent from the beginning. They are not sure what caused such a rapid turnaround in his health, and after some time it became apparent that his internal activity was slowly deteriorating. On 21st April at 7:45pm the heartbreaking decision was made to withdraw his service of care and Noah passed peacefully in Eryn's arms. Once removed from the oxygen his heart continued *to pump for a further 27 minutes, proving how strong his heart and soul are. Our beautiful first baby boy Noah has been returned to the stars where he will watch down upon the world with a smile in his eyes and a song in his heart.*

While we will never see our little guy open his eyes or hear him cry, we know that he was absolutely perfect, and that his light will shine on forever more.

Noah has been so loved in his short life that it is bittersweet to be so happy to see him so loved and yet so devastated at the same time. For those who were lucky enough to meet him, we thank you from the bottom of our hearts and hope that you will treasure his energy forever more. He really was perfect and will forever guide us all with his starlight.

Please know that we are both doing ok with the support of each other, family and close friends. Your thoughts for us and Noah will always be cherished and when we next meet if you mention his name we may be sad, but we will be much sadder if you don't.

Please, if you have children, no matter their age, show them endless love and give them a hug to last a lifetime. It will make us smile with the understanding that Noah has inspired a renewed love for one another and a deep respect for the miracle of life."

Rewind to Noah's birthday. I'm pushing Eryn in a wheelchair in a state of shock with all our family waiting outside...it was becoming too much to bear. To paraphrase Eryn and my response? "*Fucked*!" We really couldn't think of anything else to think or say.

Throughout life we learn many things. Some just stick with us for when we really need them. This was one of those times. I stopped and turned to Eryn and said, "we need to find positives here!" Not burying our head in the sand, but trying to understand what good might come of this. I have the belief that all events and behaviours have an equal number of positives as they do negatives, and it's a philosophical point of view to be sure. But how could THIS, of all things, prove that point? We would see. Over the next four days the flood came in.

The ICU team would see the largest number of visitors for one child in their memory. 70+ family and friends came to see this shooting star and would be deeply touched by him. It was very important for us for as many as possible to help us remember him always, but to also be touched by his light. His life had to mean something. There was no such thing as a waste. I would condemn anyone for suggesting it.

Grief is a funny thing. Definitely not funny 'Ha-ha' but it really is very fluid. One day it means being sad, the next you can feel like a hollow shell. The way to get through it was to remind myself of what this loss brings and being grateful that he existed. That really takes a lot of the pain away.

What are the positives? Well, I have hundreds. Literally. Where do I start?

Eryn and I are so much closer. We looked to each other for support rather than looking for someone to blame. My love and respect for Eryn after she went through this has grown immensely. I am in awe of how strong she is.

Our family is so much closer. Some who were estranged, are no longer. We are all more gentle with each other and we share Noah's memory as a family ethos. We have a saying "STOP! Noah time!" which means we need to hug the nearest person. This is also shared with many of our friends.

Our love and care for our next boy Oscar is far greater. He will grow up knowing about his older brother and what he meant to his mum and dad. Noah will be forever Oscar's guiding light.

So many friends and acquaintances, even strangers are far more ready to open up to us. I've heard so many life changing stories where I otherwise wouldn't. Eryn and I both have deeper and more meaningful conversations with others in every respect.

I am more emotional now. I know this sounds like it might be a bad thing to a guy, but I love that I can embrace the small things in life and appreciate how powerful those emotions can be.

I am also more empathetic. It makes me more tolerant when someone is having a bad day.

I could go on and on with these, but I'll finish with something that was of infinite value and I can't thank her enough. I've had the pleasure to know Helen Garrett who set up the Jake Garrett Foundation which provided financial support for funeral services to families who've lost a child. Helen has had to stop the foundation due to personal pressures but the Facebook page remains as a place for healing for those like us to share our stories and get support. Helen lost her boy Jake at 13.

The funeral, or what I decided to call a celebration of Noah's life, was attended by over 100 and we held it in the Mount Cootha Planetarium. It was perfect and the staff were great. Photos of friends and family spending time with Noah was powerful, but what made it perfect was a trail of fluffy animals in pairs leading the way to Noah. They were sending him off with all their gratitude and love.

As for all our family and friends, we are immensely grateful, but especially the Royal Brisbane Woman's Hospital staff for their amazing care and support, and of course my bestie Shelley Richter who knows no boundaries when it comes to being there for a friend. You never know how important it is to have good people in your life until you really need them.

Noah's purpose, we know now, was not to live a life and love and laugh and cry. It was, and is, to help us all be greater than we would be, to live and love and laugh and cry just that little bit more.

Andrew Purcell

Noah's purpose, we know now, was not to live a life and love and laugh and cry. It was, and is, to help us all be greater than we would be, to live and love and laugh and cry just that little bit more.

ASHLYN

On June 20, 2016, life for me changed forever. When my baby girl, Ashlyn Marie, was stillborn at 39 weeks.

I started writing soon after my daughter passed to offer myself some relief as I entered an unknown grieving process. I was trying to hold onto anything I had left of her. Any thought, any mood, any emotion. The following are excerpts from my book, but it's really her (Ashlyn) book, *Ashlyn's Journal,* which compiled a year's worth of journal entries describing my thoughts and feelings after my daughter's passing.

"When I forget the "feeling" of her, that'll be another deathblow to me. It will be like losing her all over again. I hope that day does not come soon."

When the routine of life reaches me that will be another gut shot as well. It will be like closing one chapter in my life that I desperately want to keep open in the hopes that she'll return as if this has been just a horrible nightmare. I'll wake up one day and starting a whole new chapter without her and realizing she's gone because she's not in it (and she's never coming back), that'll be like losing her all over again too." (Ashlyn's Journal, pg. 9)

I began writing getting all my thoughts out of my head and onto paper. I felt as if my head would explode if I didn't write them down. I watched my wife in such agony and seeing my daughter pass away ate at my mind and tore me up inside. I wanted her (Ashlyn) and now she was gone, I couldn't have her. I wanted my wife to be happy, I couldn't make her happy. I was useless.

"To myself:

It's ALL your fault. You can make up any excuses you want. But it's your entire fault. You could've saved her. You could've saved her and you didn't. You could've done more. Done something. Done anything. You did NOTHING. You could've saved her and you didn't.

I hate you." (Ashlyn's Journal, pg. 22)

I had to write it on paper to set it out there and out of my head or my head was going to explode. This was my way of processing what happened. I really was in such a state of denial and now still today to some degree, DENIAL, still creeps in. I just can't believe it. I can't believe this has happened.

"One in a thousand they tell us. One in a thousand like it's

supposed to make you feel better. You never think that one is going to be you. It's always someone else. Until it happens. You're the one. Ninety-nine point nine percent of the time, you're good! Well, not us. We were the one." (Ashlyn's Journal, pg. 12)

It's been over two years and I still struggle to cope with the grief. To cope with her not being here anymore. I often times go through bouts of shame, guilt, and even still more denial mixed with episodes of sadness and depression. It feels guilty to be happy. She (Ashlyn) would want me to be happy, she's my daughter and we love each other, so that makes it ok to be happy. You should feel ok, right? No, it only makes it sadder.

I continued to struggle with emotions and feelings on even the simplest of things.

"A simple question like "How are you?" has a new twist now. "How are you?" What does that even mean? How am I? How am I compared to the average person? How am I compared to how I normally feel? How am I compared to a terminally ill cancer patient? I mean, what does "how are you" even mean? Does it mean how am I compared to my usual self? Or how I think I should be? You don't know my usual self so what does my answer even mean to you? How am I? How am I supposed to be? Even the smallest questions become confusing and exhausting." (Ashlyn's Journal, pg. 15-16)

Ashlyn, my daughter in heaven, has let us know she's ok with many different signs which are explained in my book, *Ashlyn's Journal*. The biggest of which was the sudden appearance of Hummingbirds. When *Ashlyn's Journal* was written it wasn't intended to be for public. It was meant really just for me. A place I carved out to remember the thoughts and feelings that Ashlyn invoked out of me. I decided to publish, because I felt it might help people, to know they're not alone. Also, I published to preserve my ideas, and have it forever. She's been such a positive powerful presence in our lives and I wanted to share her with the rest of the world.

"I haven't been in her (Ashlyn) room in a while. I can't even remember the last time. I think today I will. The pain is still there. The image of the empty crib burning into my eyes hits my chest like a solid cold sledgehammer. I can almost hear the thud as it crushes into the center of my chest, caving in all my ribs with a sickly crunching sound. And I weep, I weep for me. I weep for a father without his daughter. This is not how I imagined her childhood would begin with an empty crib and a quiet, dark, silent, still room. But going into her room feels much worse than that, it's like a thousand hands around my throat choking me, squeezing the life out of me as my eyes swell up with tears and my nose fills with snot. I lie in the middle of the room and look around at her pictures. Her hair ties. Her furniture. Everything

is too much to bear. I get up and open her closet door. Inside I find her bassinet, which I had forgotten we stored in there. The vision of it is equally crushing as the rest of the room if not more. That bassinet was meant for her to sleep peacefully in our room, next to our bedside, not stowed away in this cold closet. Cold just like when I kissed Ashlyn's forehead as she laid in her casket at the funeral home. My eyes pour with tears and it's almost too difficult to see anything now. It's been 102 days without her and I still feel the same. That is comforting. I feel I'm beating time. Ashlyn is timeless. She was real just like how this pain now is real. She's in heaven. She has to be. If she's not, then I don't want to be either." (Ashlyn's Journal, pg. 31)

"The pain. The pain is real. And I don't try to avoid it, to run from it or push the pain away. I embrace the pain. I let the pain consume me and I wrap myself in it. For if the pain is real then so is my daughter. She is real too. It's all too easy to let the mind fade and her feel like it was a dream, a nightmare, and a distant memory. But it's not, it's real. I know because the pain is real. I remember. I embrace the pain." (Ashlyn's Journal, pg. 31)

As a parent you wonder how much you can love your kids or the next kid. It's like the Dr. Suess book, your love doesn't get halved or cut in thirds, but rather it grows twice and three times as much as I can imagine. Life is relentless. Life never stops. Life keeps on moving no matter what. Alexis is my little rainbow baby. Ashlyn was not replaced, she was only further remembered by the arrival of her little sister. Just like Ashlyn, Alexis grew this father's heart another size bigger, grew the love larger. That's what God's Love, I believe, is like for us. Billions of times grown and expanded.

It's hard to explain. The love but it's true I know. It's there because I can feel it. The wind in your hair. The sand between your toes. You can feel it. I can feel her love even more.

I still write about her. I write about her all the time. This isn't the end. This is only just the beginning.

"Your own child passing is not something you prepare for. How can you? The mere one-second thought causes too much pain to bear, when it became a reality. It was a total nightmare, in the worse sense of things. I wish I could trade places with you (Ashlyn) in an instant. But then how selfish can I be? How could I take you way from a place so beautiful, so happy, so filling with joy? And bring you into a world filled with so much darkness and despair. A world without your daddy because I traded places with you. You stay where you are, honey, my sweet angel, I'll lead a good life in your name and honor, and when God is ready we will be reunited again." (Ashlyn's Journal, pg. 19)

Love isn't a strong enough word to describe the feeling I

have for you. Over the rainbow is where I'll find you.

Love forever and always,

Your Daddy

Andrew Yackuboskey

It's hard to explain. The love but it's true I know. It's there because I can feel it. The wind in your hair. The sand between your toes. You can feel it. I can feel her love even more.

I still write about her. I write about her all the time. This isn't the end. This is only just the beginning.

Love isn't a strong enough word to describe the feeling I have for you. Over the rainbow is where I'll find you.

NOAH AND ROWAN

I've found that writing my story is a very hard thing to do. Every time I try, I find myself either giving out advice, or writing the story of my son's life, but not the story of mine. Quite often, I'll start recounting just a list of times and facts. This happened, and then this happened. And I'm not even a great story teller, so that goes nowhere fast. What I'm going to try and do instead is tell a bit of the overall story, but also tell a bit of my story. The story of how having and losing my son Noah, and then having the rest of our children, fits into my life.

My wife Louisa and I had our first child, Noah, in 2006. We'd been married for about 8 years at the time and, I, at 34, and Louisa, at 28, felt we were ready to start a family. Unfortunately, this wasn't to be. Noah was diagnosed with Spinal Muscular Atrophy (SMA) type 1 when he was 6 weeks old. The average life span for an SMA Type 1 baby was 7 months, and after a rather rapid degeneration, we lost him in April of 2007, aged just 5 month and 22 days. There is a line from a book I read once that says "You dismiss a saga in one sentence!" and the same is certainly true here. Having

Noah, caring for him through his illness, and then losing him tested me, exposed me, and tore me apart. It took me to deeper and darker places than I ever imagined existed. It was a darkness so intense it was physical, and it not only extinguished all light, but all hope, all memory of joy, and all thoughts of the possibility that one day, there could be light again. The only thing that really kept me moving through all of that was knowing that the woman by my side was going through her own personal hell and needed me desperately to hold her up when she couldn't stand, the same way I needed her to when I couldn't. At the centre of all this was our darling boy, who needed us to be there to care for him. And not only that, he needed to live a life. He had only months to live all the life he was ever going to get, and as his parents, we had to front up and be there to give him a lifetime's worth of love in just a few short months. Oddly enough, when we couldn't even hold each other up, he was actually the one who held us both up and helped us to keep going.

So we did everything in our power to give him as full a life as possible, fighting against ever increasing medical needs and restrictions. We gave him a birthday every month, because we knew how unlikely he was to reach 1 year old, and so on the 12 of each month, we had a party for him. Given that he wasn't able to move much at all, he really like to watch movies, so I made sure he got to see the original

Star Wars trilogy. He loved it and was absolutely glued to it. He also confirmed he was every bit my son when my wife, to give him a balanced exposure to cinema, put on one of her favourites, the Sound of Music. Noah proceeded to cry until she turned it off. I am being mean though, the Sound of Music is also an awesome movie, but this story is one we love telling. We also tried to take as many photos as we could, but I realize now I should have taken at least a hundred times as many as we did. I don't think we realized that, once he was gone, it really would be all we would have of him for our lifetime. Of course, even a thousand more would still not have been enough.

There were quite a few difficult times, but the day he died was one of the only times I felt like I just couldn't continue. We were at home, which was where we knew we wanted him to go, not in a cold hospital. He had been getting much worse, and struggling more and more so we knew it was close. When he did go, it was quick, and it was like he just fell asleep. We had family come and say good bye and have one last cuddle, and we held him for as long as we could, but we knew it was time to say goodbye. The funeral director had let us know that we could just lay him in his cot, close the door and he would come in and get him ready to go. I'd held it together up until that point, but as I closed the door on his room, on him, on his life, on my son, it was like the roof fell in. That first step away from his door was, without a doubt, the hardest things I have ever had to do in my life, and I struggle to imagine anything ever being that hard again. It took absolutely everything I had, every bit of emotional strength I could muster to not collapse. Again, I think knowing that Louisa was beside me, and that if I lost it, she would too, was the only thing that enabled me to take that step.

I've come to think of the people we were back then, before we had Noah, as a different set of people. Robert Pirsig in "Zen and the Art of Motorcycle Maintenance" talks about himself as two different people, the person he is now, and Phaedrus, the person he was before a massive mental break down and electric shock (electroconvulsive) therapy. We've come to think of ourselves in much the same way, barely unrecognisable. I'd read Pirsig's book long before we had Noah, and it was only on re-reading it since that the parallel really hit home for me. That losing your child is almost like the person you were has been destroyed, and it's up to you to rebuild them.

Part of the big impact that all of this has had on our lives has been that, by having Noah and him having SMA, it meant both Louisa and I carry SMA. It is a Genetic condition which is autosomal recessive. That may not mean a whole lot to most people, but what it boils down to is that any children we have will have a 1 in 4 chance of having and dying of SMA the same way Noah did. In having Noah, we were trying to start a family, and with this diagnosis, that dream just seemed further and further away. We found out that there were only a couple of options open to us. We could just not have any more children, which didn't seem to be an option for us. We could fall pregnant, test the pregnancy and terminate if the baby had SMA, or just have the child and let them die the same way Noah had. We really didn't want to face these possibilities either. Alternatively, we could do a type of IVF where the harvested eggs are fertilized, tested for SMA and then only implant the embryos that don't have SMA. This was the path we decided to go down, but after 18 months of failure after failure, and close to $50,000 spent, we couldn't continue. While trying to deal with losing Noah, the first cycle that successfully yielded a non-SMA embryo ended up in an ectopic pregnancy and Louisa losing one of her fallopian tubes. After this we had cycle after cycle where either none of the embryos survived the testing process, or a healthy embryo was implanted, only to fail to implant. The last cycle, we put in two perfectly healthy embryos, only to have neither work out, and after this, we had just run out of the emotional energy to continue, not to mention we had no money left.

We took a break, went away for a couple of days, and decided that we may have to just try naturally and take our chances. It was horrific to face the possible results of this, but we really felt like we'd been backed into a corner. The result of this leap of faith was that, after 6 weeks, we fell pregnant with a healthy, non-SMA baby. Mary was born 9 months later, and after everything that had happened, we were parents who could again hold their baby in their arms. I still feel panic sometimes when Mary is off at a sleep over somewhere, and I have to go to bed without her here close to me. The overwhelming fear of losing her is something I deal with almost daily.

We had always talked about having children, not just one child, and once Mary was old enough, we decided that we wanted to try and have another. This wasn't something we arrived at easily given what we knew was involved, and the risks, but our hearts ached for the family we wanted to hold, and raise, and love. It was then we found out that we had somehow become infertile. We tried naturally with nothing, we tried with fertility drugs and nothing, and it wasn't until we went with artificial insemination (one of the most un-romantic ways to fall pregnant let me tell you), that we had any success. This allowed us to fall pregnant with another girl Rowan. Luck wasn't with us this time though, and with a positive diagnosis of SMA, we made the heartbreaking decision to terminate. It angers me to this day, but we were and still are judged for this. In case you missed the whole beginning of this story, we love our children more than life itself. We desperately want all our children, or we wouldn't have been trying ridiculously invasive and dehumanising medical procedures to try and have one. Imagine for yourself trying to go through all of that, only to have to make the decision to then terminate the pregnancy. In a way, we were lucky. There were no chances, or odds that we had to deal with. We'd already done that and lost. We had a positive diagnosis of a fatal condition. A life that would be measured in months, and a loss that we didn't know we could survive intact. Unlike some parents who have to deal with uncertainty when faced with a decision like this, all our variables were gone. We knew what was going to happen, and we chose not to put Rowan through that. Or put Mary through watching her baby sister die. Or put us having to watch our daughter die. Or put our family through having to survive the death of another baby. And it still enrages me that we were judged for it. That people felt justified in standing in judgement of us and telling my wife she would go to hell, as if we hadn't been there already.

We had twice walked out of the same hospital with a beautiful newborn baby. I never stood as tall and as proud as walking beside my amazing wife, a new mother who looked both radiant and the picture of happiness. So let me tell you that then walking out of that maternity hospital, cuddling my wife to me who has just had to deliver and say goodbye to another baby, another bitterly wanted and already dearly loved baby, with nothing in our arms and nothing to show but anguish, was way up on that list of low points in my life. And people think we chose to do that because we were weak.

And yet, we had to try again. It sounds almost ridiculous to say it here, and it's not to say that we didn't talk and think and discuss and talk with our counsellor about our decision. The same reasons still held true, and to stop at this point would have felt somehow like saying that Rowan's life had in some way not meant anything. So after more fertility and going back again to artificial insemination (just how many people should be in the room when you fall pregnant?) we fell pregnant with Emmaline. Emmaline is a keeper, her testing came up clear, and after a few issues with the pregnancy, she joined our family, and at 5 years old, is right now sleeping in the room with her big sister.

And that brings me to today. We are a family. We have our ups and downs, and sometimes, with what we've been through, we can maybe struggle a little more with life's challenges because of the load we are carrying. Time hasn't reduced the weight of the losses we have suffered, I like to think that we have become stronger in order to carry them. Sure, we are a bit slower up the hills and stairways of life because of them. We may not be as quick of step as we could be, but for the most part, we're proud of what and who we carry with us.

People don't look at me and realize that we have a shelf in our bedroom that has two baby urns on it for the two children we have lost. It's too sad for them. Sometimes, it's too sad for us as well, but that's our life. Mary and Emmaline bring us immense joy and laughter. I can't imagine my life without them, or without my wife who has been my rock and my inspiration.

Brett Carter

We are a family. We have our ups and downs, and sometimes, with what we've been through, we can maybe struggle a little more with life's challenges because of the load we are carrying. Time hasn't reduced the weight of the losses we have suffered, I like to think that we have become stronger in order to carry them. Sure, we are a bit slower up the hills and stairways of life because of them. We may not be as quick of step as we could be, but for the most part, we're proud of what and who we carry with us.

PERSEPHONEE

Persephonee Norma Nefzger Banks, my little P, was my everything. She was easily the most beautiful thing I have ever seen and was far and wide the best thing I have ever done. She was born on July 17th, 2009 and left us on February 26th, 2015. She was 5 ½ according to her very accurate math and on pace to continue to amaze me every day. She had started Kindergarten in the fall and loved school. She was an only child, so playing with friends made her day. She was learning Spanish, could count to 119, and knew the order of the planets in our solar system. She had the most infectious giggle and laugh and was extraordinarily ticklish. She loved Disney Princesses and said she was going to either be; a Princess Doctor, a Princess Lawyer, or a Math / Gym / Spanish teacher when she grew up. She could have done whatever she wanted in life. She was kind to friends and loved her little cousins. She shared everything, offering you her last piece of candy if you wanted it. She was my little gamer and loved playing video games. Mom and her played Zelda together, her and I build worlds and chased after one another in Disney Infinity, and we all played Super Mario

Brothers as a family. The times we spent building a new town or trying to collect all the stars were more important to me than any of my past achievements combined. I'd trade every one of them for a chance to hold her in my arms again and feel her little hands clasp behind mine in a gabble grip.

So what happened? Why was she taken from us with so much fucking potential? February 20th, we sent the girl over to Ya-Ya's (Grand-ma's) for the evening. It was a Friday, we're going to have a date night at a movie. She loved Ya-Ya's place and would have spent a week there had we let her. She was spoiled by her grandparents, of course, but also just loved experiencing and living. That night she said her throat hurt a little, but she was in good spirits.

In the morning she wasn't feeling great. Mom gave her some meds and we spent the day resting and playing video games downstairs. That night at bedtime she said she was having a little trouble breathing when she laid down. I figured it was typical, how it's harder to breathe easily when you are sick and congested and lying flat. So, she sat in my lap on the couch and fell asleep watching one of her shows on Sprout. After she fell asleep I put her to bed and she curled up, sleeping soundly. After that she was up all night with her mom. Around 5:00 in the morning she was having such a hard time breathing that she was pacing the floor. So we raced her to the emergency room. We spent all Sunday in the hospital. The doctors gave her a Nebulizer and put in an IV, which she was not happy with. They took X-rays and she began to feel better. Around 5:00 or so we were released as the doctor was pretty sure she had croup. We were told to keep an eye on her at home and got some meds for her.

The rest is a nightmare. I see it when I fall asleep at night and feel it when I wake up in the morning. It hurts. I try to push the memory and picture her jumping into my arms laughing, but it still hurts so much.

Persephonee started having trouble breathing again so I grabbed her in my arms and raced outside. We live in Minnesota and the doctor told us the cold air would make her feel better. Outside the air was so cold, I asked her to take slow, small breaths. When we got outside I watched her eyes roll backyards and yelled for her to stay with me. I didn't know it then, but her little heart was having a heart attack. The First Responders were there within two or three minutes and took over. They tried. After twenty-one minutes they got the airway open and a pulse. Twenty minutes too late. I don't want to go into the rest.

After being at the hospital for a couple of days, the doctor came to talk with us. We stood holding Persephonee's had and she said the eight words that I hear in my dreams. "I believe your daughter is going to die." I yelled and fell down, the wall fell back and I sobbed. The doctor knew, as I knew in my heart, my baby was gone. I'm not sure how Amee reacted. I think she was numb with shock. I eventually got to my feet and held her as tight as I could. We cried, as we cry just about every day now. I miss her so much.

Somewhere along the way my wife and I decided together that she would donate her organs, try to save others. Maybe that made it feel like it gave her death more meaning, but it didn't feel that way. It just hurt. We were in the hospital the next two days trying to give as much time as we could for ideal circumstances for her gifting. February 26th became her Gifting Day. I'm not sure who came up with the term, Amee, or if it existed before, but it felt much better than the day my world grew dark.

My life is now a series of Firsts. Things that I've done a thousand times over my life, but never like this. That first night in the house without her was so quiet. She always slept with a fan or dehumidifier on in her room down the hall. Lying in bed before sleep I would hear it as well. The house was so still I couldn't sleep much.

The next morning, I woke before the sun and opened her bedroom door, like I've done a million times. She wasn't in her big girl bed like she was supposed to be. We each chose a favorite animal of hers to sleep with. Amee took Susan, one of her first and favorite Penguins, I took Sally, a small tabby cat named after Amee's first cat when she was a little girl. We still sleep with them. Sometimes I'll wake up a few hours after I fall asleep and reach up for Sally, pulling her tight against my chest. It's not P, but it feels like a part of her.

Sometime in the next few weeks we needed groceries and decided to stop at the grocery store for supplies. Another painful first. We went in and Amee immediately got some fruit. We then walked over to the dairy section and both stopped. What did we need? Nothing here seemed necessary anymore. Our shopping was always designed around Persephonee. What would the girl have in her lunches, what would we make for family meals, what kind of snacks of hers are low. So what did we need now? Amee and I held each other in the dairy isle, next to the cereal for sale and cried. I held on longer then I think she needed, but I needed more. I'm sure people were confused, but honestly, I never saw any of them. I just cried and held my wife. Eventually we grabbed a few more unnecessary items and fled the store.

My life is now this, a million firsts, just as I'm sure your life is now a million stupid firsts. Any store I go into reminds me of her. I'm vulnerable at every point where my life intersected hers. Movies, candies, foods, shows, commercials, animals, roads, even fucking clouds, everything is tied to her in some way and hurts. Everything. They come at the least expectant of times. Last night I was in a good place, Amee and I were out and looking for a snack. I found some on sale Easter candy, which lead me to a candy isle, where I saw a Necco Waffers, the image of which fired some long torment neurons on my brain and conjured up the memory of me and P buying them at a gas station. That night we made a fort in the living room and watched a movie while we feasted on snacks, highlighted by her first Necco Waffers.

I don't ever want to forget her or the things we did, so I let the Firsts wash over me and bathe in the painful memories. At those times she feels a little closer to me. Some of them I share with Amee or those around me, some are just for me. Regardless, I know they are coming, so I look for them and when they hit, I remember life and why it was so fun.

I need to face the facts, I'm no longer who I was. At a fundamental level, I am no longer me. This kills me. I loved who I was. I loved who she made me. I loved who I was with and because of her. This new person, this new thing that exists, but isn't like before, I don't love it. But what can I do, because it is now me. Chris AP (after Persephonee) wants to talk about his daughter a lot, but can only share old stories, things from by-gone days. It hurts him to talk about her, but the alternative hurts more. He misses watching her shows with her, but can't, it's too painful.

The new me scares me. It scares me because I know I'm a different person. The person all my friends liked, the person I was known as, the person my wife fell in love with, he's been replaced by this fragile, underdeveloped doppelganger.

I continue on in my new form with my new reality. It will never get less painful, especially if I dwell on what I've lost, it will just get less frequent. But even that feels like a betrayal of her. I tell myself it's not, and that laughter, life, and happiness were her things, they should be mine too. It's just hard. I miss my little girl. I honestly don't think there is getting through this, just living with it. Amee says we are surviving it, not moving through it. I agree, there are no stages and is no getting over it, it will always be and living with it in a way that honors her is what is important.

I've come to discover that my emotions are tied closely to one another. Sadness and happiness, disappointment and anger, love and anguish, one is so close to the other that they often spill out together or even co-exist simultaneously. Lying in bed at night my mind will turn to despair and sorry, so I'll instead turn to a memory of P and me laughing together. That memory though, so full of happiness, resides with dismal heartbreak. So instead I exist in sorrowful joy, painful bliss, and delightful anguish. I'll keep feeling, keep hurting, keep knowing that my baby is both here and gone.

Through all of this I've felt guilty at the level of support we've gotten from people. I've always prided myself on being fairly self-sufficient. One of the driving factors for entering the Marines when I was eightteen was so that the family no longer had to support me. So the amazing outpouring of love and kindness we've had through all of this gives me a little trepidation. It shouldn't, I know, people are doing what they can because there is nothing else to do, but it still does.

I'm not sure what support works and what doesn't. It's different for everyone. I like to talk about her and share her. Amee likes being around her friends, filling up her schedule with something to do. I do know that the little things people did and do for me mean a lot. Bringing a drink, even from the next room, bringing dinner now that our dining table seems so empty, calling to meet up because they know I won't, offering company and companionship. Some friends don't feel like they should or that they are being intrusive, but right now, it's all we have. All I can suggest is find the support you need and cling to it, for as long as you need. There is no wrong way or right way to live now, it's just survival. I want my survival to stand for Persephonee, but that's just me. Find what yours is for and latch on, it might give life a little more meaning. Again, there is no getting through or past this. It's my new existence and will be for as long as I am. At times that is a daunting notion, to know that I will always feel this pain, always be vulnerable. The truth is though, it was always a possibility, it just loomed far out at sea, a massive ship tiny on the horizon. Sometimes the ship gets a bit closer, other times it moves further out in the water, but it's always there, never gone. The SS Persephonee, my ever constant, beautiful reminder.

Christopher Banks

I've come to discover that my emotions are tied closely to one another. Sadness and happiness, disappointment and anger, love and anguish, one is so close to the other that they often spill out together or even co-exist simultaneously. I exist in sorrowful joy, painful bliss, and delightful anguish. I'll keep feeling, keep hurting, keep knowing that my baby is both here and gone.

LENNI

I am never sure if Lenni's birth was the end or the beginning. I find it hard to differentiate between the two. She was unexpectedly dead shortly before she was born and with that discovery our whole world fell apart. I remember the feeling was like sky diving down a ravine with the only surety being that the rocky ground would be there to greet me with its sharp impact sooner or later. Our world closed in and we were shut in an opaque bubble of shock and grief. The noises that we heard whilst in the hospital delivering and caring for our dead daughter whilst she was still there in body haunted us for a long time after. The air had been punctuated by the noises of labouring mums, proud new dads, the rhythmic pounding of CTGs and the fresh screams of newborn infants. That night had not been soundproofed and this facet of our experience turned later into part of my mission as a gladiator for the rights and quality of care for stillborn parents and their babies.

I guess a good place to start would be to explain that I am a fun loving person who met his soulmate, my fun loving wife to fall in love under the stars and the full moon in Thailand.

We didn't have a care in the world as we went backpacking together. We soon moved in together, bought a house and got married. We were part of a community, had a large friendship group and were involved in a wide variety of local projects and hobbies. Music filled our lives and our zest for life and fun filled our days. We had our first baby, a son called Malakai in 2003, our second, a daughter called Jaime soon followed in 2005. Life got hectic and we made fantastic memories every day. When I wasn't working I came home, loving our growing family and basking in the experience of being a dad within our growing family.

We loved it so much that we decided to carry on having more children. This is when disaster struck. Lisa had 2 miscarriages, at 12 and 10 weeks. We were gutted by the seemingly cruel randomness with which death and loss had struck. We went for some medical advice and were told that the recurrent miscarriage clinic required you to have three miscarriages to gain access to this kind of care. So after much soul searching, discussion, depression and the loss of romance, we tried again. We not as quick to become pregnant this time and every month when we found out that we were not, struck us more and more harshly. Eventually we did become pregnant again and everything was going so well. Shortly before the birth, under the care of a private midwife we found that there was no heartbeat and after being rushed into hospital, Lenni was born.

"With great sadness, we welcome Lenni Veronica Shaffer into the world, born without taking her first breath. We thank you in advance for your well wishes"

I was crushed beyond how I could imagine anyone could feel. Within 24 hours, according to our Jewish tradition, we stood at her graveside, committing her body to the ground in a coffin, the size of which betrayed its contents. My daughter, Lenni, instead of being in the warmth of our embrace, being seized by the cold damp of freshly dug soil and all that we could hold was a palpable emptiness, unfairly represented by the shattered fragments of our hopes and dreams.

We decided not to have a post mortem as it would have meant cutting up our dead daughter and we felt that we didn't want to do that. We went back for a meeting with the consultant and head midwife, they had no answers and we found that not a lot could have been done to save her apart from perhaps having an early planned caesarian. We questioned ourselves and still do about why we were so adamant about having a home birth and going till full term. The reality is that the birth decisions we made were not outrageous even in hindsight. However, that doesn't stop us feeling regular guilt about the fact that our decisions killed our daughter. We have discussed this together many times. In common with many other bereaved parents we still live with this guilt.

We went back to the recurrent miscarriage clinic, thinking we had earned the right to care under their terms. We were told that a stillbirth doesn't count as a miscarriage. The doors were shut to us once again. We still had the urge to have more children. Our living children were so precious to us that we didn't want to become obsessive but our drive to have more children spurned us on. We became pregnant once again or at least we suspected it. Lisa did a pregnancy test and put the test stick in the bathroom cabinet. It was 4 weeks before i gave in to have a look at the result. We were so scared of being pregnant and so scared of not being pregnant. The two blue lines were there and as I saw them I realised that this was not happy relief. This was only the beginning of the hour by hour worry that dragged on through months of painful waiting and worry. I realised that nothing would ever be the same again. We had lost our happy go lucky innocence of being in the pregnancy bubble. Ours was a world where things could go wrong for no apparent reason at any time.

Optimism was replaced with an all devouring fear. In the end though a boy, Ziggy, was born by early planned caesarian section. With his birth came an unexpected resurgence of grief. We once again mourned the loss of what we should have had with Lenni and then felt guilty about not being able to feel the intense joy at Ziggy's birth. For the first six months of his life, we didn't put him down, kangaroo caring at all times and adoring him in very overprotective ways. We catastrophized every normal sniffle into life changing illness but somehow managed to regain a 'normal' sense of living with our beautiful family.

We were still not done and after much debate, decided to try again. Reproduction was a lot more mechanical now but we managed to conceive and after a pretty uneventful pregnancy Keanu, another son was born alive and healthy. Three miscarriages followed and then I made the decision for the sake of Lisa's mental health to have a vasectomy. Ten years and ten pregnancies was enough for our reproductive story in our family. We could now start to regain ourselves.

I sit here writing this as my youngest son is 7 years old. Lenni is talked about often in our family and every Friday night without fail we raise a glass to her. She has had such far reaching consequences for us and our family and friends. Tens of thousands of pounds have been raised in her name, we have climbed mountains for her, collected old clothes for her.

2 years after Lenni was born we started to go to a parent support group with SANDS. We ended up running the group for four years and I am still active in running the local branch of this charity. I have become a bereavement care trainer, going in to hospitals to help professional teams deliver gold standard care to the parents who experience the death of their babies shortly before during or after birth.

Every year on Lenni's birthday we go away somewhere together for a 'Yes weekend' where if the children ask something they know the answer can only be yes, they eat sweets for breakfast, buy skateboards and t shirts and all in the name of having fun in Lenni's name.

Lenni was not alive outside of the womb to leave her footprints on this earth so we do this for her. Every footprint leaves an indelible impact for Lenni on this earth and we carry on leaving footprints in her name. We form our lives around our loss and we are all richer for her existence. In other people's minds she might have existed in the past. For us, her existence spurns us on to bigger and greater things. I hope that sharing this experience brings strength and hope to anyone that reads it. Even though a baby's death seems like a cruel end, it is often only the beginning of great things to come. I never realised I could do half the things that I have done. Lenni is my strength, she would have done amazing, earth shattering things so for her, my family does everything we do to leave indelible footprints on this earth.

We all have mountains to climb. Some days we manage it and sometimes we don't. The most important thing, however, is to pick ourselves up tomorrow and try again.

Dan Shaffer

Lenni was not alive outside of the womb to leave her footprints on this earth so we do this for her. Every footprint leaves an indelible impact for Lenni on this earth and we carry on leaving footprints in her name. We form our lives around our loss and we are all richer for her existence.

AUBREY VIOLET

Weeks leading up to the birth of Aubrey Violet were stressful for my wife and me. My wife Colleen was put on bed rest at 23 weeks. Seeing your loved one in bed with your soon to be first child was nerve-wrecking.

Then, I received a phone call from work that would change our lives forever. I remember picking up the phone and Colleen saying, "You need to come to the hospital now they are going to deliver Aubrey Violet." I hung up the phone and called my supervisor telling him I needed to go to the hospital.

As I raced to the hospital, which was about 25 minutes away, I remember feeling a lot of emotions. I felt anxious, excited, nervous, and scared to list a few. When I finally arrived at the hospital I hurried up to the room and remember looking at Colleen's face with excitement but uncertainty as well. I remember feeling nervous, but needed to stay strong for Colleen.

When they delivered Aubrey, we didn't hear her cry and didn't see her. The nurses took her to the NICU right away.

I recall one of the nurses saying, "Do you see that?" I am not sure if Colleen heard this, but I didn't feel good when I heard that. I felt that there was something wrong. About an hour later we got to see Aubrey. Aubrey was hooked up to a bunch of monitors and had glasses on. She only weighed little over a pound. My sister-in-law, Rachael was born early weighing a pound and is perfectly healthy. Seeing Aubrey in her glass box with all the monitors hooked up to her, I felt that she was in the right place and that she was in the care of the best doctors and nurses for her to make it. I couldn't believe I was a Dad.

Going back to see Aubrey Violet and Colleen was tough. I recall trying to be positive for Colleen and then going back to see how Aubrey was doing. There was a lot of back and forth between rooms that day. I am very thankful for our family and friends because they were all there for us. Finally, at about midnight, Colleen and I decided to go to bed and get some rest. The nurses and doctors at this time said that Aubrey's oxygen levels were getting better and that we should get some rest, so we did.

The next day on May 29th, 2015, the doctor came into the room and woke us up. Colleen and I were both in shock and nervous. The doctor said throughout the night they had to revive Aubrey Violet and her oxygen levels were declining.

At this point we didn't have the time to research or know what to do. So, Colleen asked the doctor, "If this was your child what would you do?" The doctor said, "If this was my child I would want to hold her and spend as much time with her before she took her last breath." At this time our immediate family was there, and we wanted to hold her. The doctor said that there was some bleeding in the brain and at this point they did everything they could to help her and they didn't know when she was going to take her last breath.

This was the toughest day of my life. As Colleen and I were holding her we just hugged her and gave her kisses. My step-daughter Ellie, my mom, sister, brother-in-law, sister-in-law, mother-in-law, and father-in-law were all in the room. We all were very emotional. I remember holding Aubrey crying and saying, "I just wanted to be your Dad." I believe Aubrey took her last breath when Colleen was holding her. Words fail how hard that was for me and my family.

Aubrey was so beautiful. She had long legs, fingers, and toes like me. When she passed we wanted to have pictures of her, so we had some beautiful pictures of her dressed up. We decided that we wanted to give her a service and she was going to be buried with her family. I recall going to the mall and wanting to buy items to put in her casket. I went to the baby girl section and seeing all the Daddy shirts my emotions got the best of me and I couldn't stop tearing up. I went to a jewelry store and found something perfect. We associate Aubrey with purple, so I bought her a necklace with a purple heart on it to wear. We had the service less than a week later with only immediate family and close friends. My in-laws had everyone over to watch the photos the hospital took on a slide show and celebrate Aubrey's life.

Looking back, that was tough for me to do but I am glad we did it. Days after I remember being depressed and angry at God. I wanted to be strong and positive for Colleen, but I was angry. I tried to be supportive, but would often find myself fighting with Colleen about miscellaneous things around the house. Colleen would stay in our room and I would go to my mancave area and eat everything I could get my hands on and watch a lot of TV and movies. I rarely went to the gym and would often take naps. I believe everyone had vices and I went to some of my vices to cope with my depression. I was grieving in a negative way. I would put on a positive face when I was around Colleen, but deep down inside I was hurting. I gained about 40 pounds. I always weighed around 220 pounds, but I was 258.

The turning point of me grieving came from a drive home after an interview. I was listening to a Christian radio station K-Love and a song came on by Tenth Avenue North called, "By Your Side" this song changed my life. During this song I felt that Aubrey was speaking to me and saying, "Dad, I will always be by your side." I have never cried before listening to a song but after this song I was covered in tears. I felt a sense of peace after hearing this song and my feelings for God and feeling that Aubrey was in Heaven and that we would see her again. Later that night I went on the treadmill and walked and ran for about 30 minutes, I almost burned 500 calories. I told myself that I wanted to get healthy and fit again and I would dedicate my workouts for Aubrey Violet. I would have her birthday, 5/28, in my head and I would burn 528 calories 3-4 times a week. I would also do reps for her totaling up to 28 reps. At the gym I would listen to "By Your Side" on the treadmill and often look at the picture of me kissing Aubrey Violet and I would blow her kisses. I was able to lose about 40 pounds the healthy way through the course of several months.

I shared my story with an editor at Men's Health and they published my article dedicated to Aubrey Violet. After the magazine was published I wanted to continue honoring Aubrey Violet by helping others. With the help of my partner Bill and graphic/web designer Sooji, we created *Dads of Steele*. A health and wellness company geared toward Dads being the best version of themselves for their families.

Instead of being bitter for the rest of my life and probably getting divorced and living a life of depression, I wanted to be better and live for Aubrey. *Dads of Steele* focuses on family, faith, and fitness the same pillars that gets me through the daily grief of losing Aubrey. I also wanted to share that anyone that deals with a loss when you're ready be mindful of the signs your loved ones send your way.

Within the same year of Aubrey being born we were blessed with Madelyn Rose. At around 16 months, I would take Madelyn to a soccer class. The first time the soccer coach gave everyone a stamp, that day he gave all the kids a purple heart stamp. That was special, Aubrey Violet was saying, "Hello" to us. Colleen and I bought a new SUV we received a new license plate. When the guy gave me the license plate and when you think about all the different combinations with letters and numbers it's a lot. I received a license plate with the first two and only letters being AS (Aubrey Steele).

Aubrey Violet, you are a beautiful angel in heaven. You are the superhero behind *Dads of Steele* and making the world a better place.

Love, Daddy

David Steele

The turning point of me grieving came from a drive home after an interview. I was listening to a Christian radio station K-Love and a song came on by Tenth Avenue North called, "By Your Side" this song changed my life. During this song I felt that Aubrey was speaking to me and saying, "Dad, I will always be by your side." I have never cried before listening to a song but after this song I was covered in tears. I felt a sense of peace after hearing this song and my feelings for God and feeling that Aubrey was in Heaven and that we would see her again.

BRYSON

It has been 8 years since I last held my son. Bryson was delivered early due to medical complications at 20 weeks, and I will never forget the few short hours I shared with him.

My wife and I had been married for almost 4 years before we finally were pregnant. We knew we wanted children from the beginning and had the mistaken notion it would be easy to start a family. After many tests and many tears, we were finally pregnant! Cautiously optimistic we had an uneventful 4 /12 months of pregnancy. Our ultrasound was scheduled and we were ready to find out the gender of our long awaited baby.

But we never made it to the appointment. At around 19 weeks my wife started to deliver and we didn't know why. We had a few tough weeks in and out of the hospital leading up to the day we lost him. We had been admitted to the hospital; it was late at night and the phone beside my wife's hospital bed rang. It was our doctor, telling us we could no longer wait and hold out for a miracle – he had to be delivered, now. Nothing could have prepared a young father expecting his first child for the next few hours. I looked on helpless as a team of medical staff gathered around my wife and began the delivery process. My heart broke into three pieces. 1 for my wife, 1 for my son, and 1 for me. I couldn't do anything but simply hold her hand.

Minutes that seemed like hours finally passed, and the doctor handed me a small baby boy who hours before flipped happily around on the ultrasound, now lay lifeless. He had 10 fingers, 10 toes, and a face that had features of me and her. It wasn't the delivery I expected, but I immediately fell in love, while at the same time I was crushed. There in my hands was my future, my hopes, my dreams. As I watched my wife, I could see the same mixed emotions, and I didn't know quite what to say. I took in every minute, watching her with our son. Seeing the love only a mother can possess for her child. Then it was time to say goodbye, and just like that he came into our life and left. Too short, too lifeless, too painful.

My wife and I spent hours in the hospital trying to process what just happened. Luckily (at least I felt lucky at the time) a feeling of shock was helping to keep the deep emotions from surfacing. Over time, I am not so sure the shock was good, as I buried a lot of grief deep in my soul. I couldn't begin to think about never seeing him smile, never hearing him laugh, and never holding my hand. I just couldn't face what might have been with his little life.

Over the next few days we had many people reach out to express love and sympathy. It seemed as though no one knew quite what to say. We were just holding on to each other, and doing the best that we could to be strong for one another. I could see it in her eyes day after day, the pain behind her smile. My heart was breaking, as I wanted to be the person to protect her, and be strong for her. I did the best that I could and gave her everything I could. I was trying to keep my own feelings inside so I could give more to her. I remember many days crying on my way to work, as I found it to be an outlet for the pain I didn't want to share with her. I could see she was already carrying more than any Mom should.

We talked all the time, and found our love was strong. But we always knew there was a deeper conversation that needed to take place. There were times when she was ready, and I wasn't. There were times I was ready, and she wasn't. Finally, one afternoon while standing in our kitchen the emotions that we had held in regarding our son came to the surface. I cried as I told my wife I couldn't be there for her in an emotional support way, because I was broken inside.

I had tried and gave it my all, but I couldn't any longer. She wept and let me know I didn't have to carry it all, and we should carry the weight together. Admitting to her that I had been hurting was the moment I started to be able to process all that had happened in the last few months.

We knew we needed help from others, and from that moment on decided it was time to let people into our life. When asked how I was doing, I would be honest and it would vary day to day. I found that I had many friends that were there for me, and although didn't know what to say – I could see that they cared. It allowed me more strength to share with my wife. All I ever wanted was to give her everything, and,unfortunately, I couldn't fix this. I couldn't work more hours, I couldn't give more time, I could simply give her my hand and promise it would be okay. Someday.

Someday hasn't come, but over the last 8 years we have had many experiences that have brought my wife and I closer together, and closer to Bryson (our son). We have felt his presence over and over again, and done our best to honor his name. We have celebrated his birthday, given away his Christmas each year to someone in need, and served other parents who are going through loss. During a remembrance ceremony, I was asked to share a quick thought on a Father's perspective, and here are the words I wrote:

A Dad's Perspective:

When I thought about my perspective as a Dad, I realized mine has evolved and changed with time.

A perspective then:

I always pictured myself as the protector, especially a protector of my wife, and my children. I never thought I would know what it was like to be so helpless, but when I lost my son – I very quickly realized I didn't have the power to protect my wife from the physical or emotional pain, and I couldn't save my son...I struggled to simply save myself.

A loss of child hurts like nothing else, because I was constantly lost in thoughts of what might have been.

I looked down at my hands, and there was no baby to hold.

When I held out my finger, there was no small hand to reach for it.

When I went to bed, there was a kiss goodnight left on my lips.

My perspective then was filled with loss, and loneliness. Although there were many friends and family who were by my side, I couldn't stop thinking about what I was going to miss. I missed my son.

A perspective now:

I am a very different person than I was then. The loss of a child changed me. In many ways I am a better person, as I have a unique perspective on life, love and loss. I still have moments where I am jaded by the circumstances of this life, but I push through and remember that I can live every day in a way that would make Bryson proud.

He would be seven years old, and as a Dad, I focus on moments – precious moments missed with my son. I have already missed his first word, his first step, and his first day of school. I have missed us playing catch for the first time, and I have missed many bedtime stories.

Although there are many things that I have missed, there are many things I haven't missed because of Bryson. I haven't missed an opportunity to love someone in time of need. I haven't missed a chance to cry with a friend. I haven't missed saying I love you, and I haven't missed opportunities to serve in his memory. And the list goes on. I thought my list would have more manly things, but Bryson made my heart soft.

I have also been able to watch my wife heal, and heal others. I have watched quietly as she has given of her time and talents, and found love and strength in others. As a spouse, there is a special bond as hearts heal together.

I will always love my son, and have hope knowing that he

touched my life for good. I wouldn't trade my 4 hours with him for anything, as it was that little lifeless body that taught me so much more about love than I could ever know.

I have since had many experiences where I have felt his presence, his love, and had the opportunity to love others with a love that is unique to those in this room.

To those in this room that are remembering a son or a daughter, may their remembrance bring love – and may love bring healing.

I will never forget the 10 fingers and 10 toes that made this man the happiest Dad, even if it was only 4 short hours. Bryson Graham Thompson, I love you, and your Mom and I will never stop missing you.

www.thetearsfoundation.org/newhampshire

Graham Thompson

Although there are many things that I have missed, there are many things I haven't missed because of Bryson. I haven't missed an opportunity to love someone in time of need. I haven't missed a chance to cry with a friend. I haven't missed saying I love you, and I haven't missed opportunities to serve in his memory. And the list goes on. I thought my list would have more manly things, but Bryson made my heart soft.

LOGAN

It's hard to write a story that you have never told. A story you've thought about every day for close to four years but have never shared with anyone - even those closest to you. This is a story that has no ending as it continues to impact every day of my life. My first born, Logan, was born on December 18, 2014 at 24 gestational weeks. He passed away shortly after his birth. The impact on my wife, Maddie, and I was considerable.

When I think about Logan I don't start by thinking about the events of December 18th. I start by thinking of a time a few weeks prior. It was a crisp November night and I was letting our dog out before going to bed. I stood under the stars playing fetch with him and I thought about how lucky I was. I was married to the love of my life. We had purchased our second home together the past Spring. The home that we planned on raising our family in. Maddie and I both had jobs that we enjoyed. I remember thinking about how fortunate I was having never experienced a significant tragedy in life. I often think I wouldn't have thought that.

The morning of December 18th started with Maddie feeling some discomfort on and off. She went to work and called her doctor, who schedule her for an appointment for the afternoon. Maddie ended up going home early from work. She kept me updated throughout the morning at around 11:45 she told me she planned on going to the ER as discomfort had gotten worse. I left work in order to bring Maddie to the doctor (my work was only 10 blocks from our house). I opened the garage door as I pulled into our driveway and when I got out of my truck, I could hear Maddie screaming in pain. Her water had broken in our kitchen. We rushed to the hospital which was a short distance away.

Logan was born around 12:15pm with a heart-beat, but he was not breathing. We watched as medical personnel, some of which I knew personally, attempted to revive Logan for half an hour before he officially passed on at 12:45pm. I have never felt so helpless in my life.

It's difficult to put into words my thoughts and feelings in the days, weeks, months, and years since Logan's death. It is easier to talk about how his death impacted by wife, our families, and friends. Ultimately, this is because it allows me to distance myself from my own feelings. The two more prevalent emotions, besides utter sadness, immediately following his death were of a loss of control and inadequacy.

I often felt inadequate as a partner because I wasn't able to make Maddie "feel better." I wanted to fix it so she didn't have to suffer or feel sad, I couldn't. While in labor Maddie kept saying she was sorry. I honestly don't know if she even remembers saying it. I did my best to assure her she had nothing to be sorry about it, but for months after Logan's death I questioned what kind of partner I had been that my wife felt the need to apologize to me for what happened. Intellectually I knew this feeling wasn't rationale, but I still felt it. I wanted to do whatever I could to make Maddie feel better. I eventually realized she was strong enough to do this on her own.

The feeling of loss of control, I believe, significantly damaged my mental health and relationships for years after Logan's death. I first felt this way when I went home from the hospital to change the day Logan died. I cried and punched everything I could. I apologized to him because I wasn't able to protect him. One night after we returned from the hospital Maddie told me she needed me to be strong for her. How I lived out this request was not healthy. I did my best to stuff and hide any emotion that wasn't "strong." She needed me to be there and support her. I was, but I also tried to become emotionless. I simply acted out my emotions differently. This isn't what she wanted and I knew it, but it gave me control over something.

I sought to gain control in any means possible. This proved to be unhealthy. The most damaging thing I did, I believe, was how I attempted to prepare for future negative events. I am, and always have been, a firm believer in visualization. I spent countless hours imaging terrible things happening, from Maddie dying (and later our children), family members being injured, accidents at work, to encountering tragic accidents in the world. I attempted to mentally prepare myself to how I would respond to these situations. I didn't want to be caught off guard again. I became paranoid and anxious. I remember a time, years later, when Maddie was late coming home with our son. I called her a few times and she didn't answer. I paced throughout our house and eventually resigned myself to the fact that they had been in a terrible car accident and died. She came home a few minutes later. I've never told anyone I did this.

As a result of these feelings I chose to go on my grief journey alone. I didn't know how to grieve and I wasn't comfortable enough with my emotions. I stumbled through it. What happened with Logan was tragic. I didn't want to negatively impact others by talking about him or what I was going through. I was more worried about other's feelings than my own. I thought I could go through it alone. This isn't to say that I had to do it alone. There were people that would have been there for me (Maddie especially), but I made a conscious decision to not seek help. I didn't want to burden anyone. They needed to grieve and I didn't want my grief to get in the way. People would often offer help or say to let them know if I needed anything. I appreciated the gesture but knew I wouldn't ever take them up of their offer. I needed to be pushed. Most people wouldn't push. The ones that did knew too well the pain I was going through.

Many people do not know how to act around those experiencing grief. This was incredibly disheartening. You expect people to act in a certain way and when they don't you end up getting hurt. I wish I wouldn't have had expectations for how some people would respond. Lots of people, both family and friends, acted in ways that I wouldn't have expected. This was both a positive and negative. Some people were simply good at being present and not shying away. Others were simply inconsiderate. A few months after we lost Logan, my brother and his wife announced they were having their second child by surprising the whole family at a birthday party. Maddie and I were grieving and ended up leaving the party in tears. We received an apology over text that, in part, stated they didn't think we would respond that way. The apology could have stopped at "we didn't think."

I've learn to accept and live with what happened. I'm not scared of my emotions anymore. I've dealt with the loss of control by understanding we can't control what happens to us, but we can control how we respond. Worrying is pointless. I wish I could go back and do things differently. I would get professional help or take advantage of the help that was available to me. I would worry less about how my feelings would impact others. Most importantly, I would change how I acted towards my Maddie. She needed me to be strong, but she also needed me to be human. My choices denied us the ability to go on our full grief experience together.

This isn't a story without a happy ending. Maddie and I now have two young boys after two high risk pregnancies. We eventually talked about my feelings. Logan's death served as a motivator for me to go graduate school. We celebrate Logan every year on his birthday. Maddie and I have both learned more about ourselves and our relationship is stronger than it was before. We've reached out and tried to support other people that have had similar tragedies happen.

Joe Babcock

It's difficult to put into words my thoughts and feelings in the days, weeks, months, and years since Logan's death. It is easier to talk about how his death impacted by wife, our families, and friends. Ultimately, this is because it allows me to distance myself from my own feelings. The two more prevalent emotions, besides utter sadness, immediately following his death were of a loss of control and inadequacy.

LILLIAN

Lillie is my little girl who died at 35 weeks, just one month shy of her due date. As I write this, I am less than a week from her second birthday, which is really the day she was stillborn. I remember almost everything from the two days that so quickly came apart so clearly that it may as well have been a week since her passing.

I never knew that a hurt this profound could even exist, nor for so long. My daughter was someone I dreamt about so often during my wife's pregnancy. It hurts to think about how many more stories I could have read to her when she was in the womb, but nothing hurts as much as knowing that those brief moments when she was a growing baby in her mother are the only tangible parts of her life I will ever have. Despite her passing, Lillian is included everywhere in our lives, but her physical absence is still abundantly evident.

One of the biggest wounds I have experienced is the apparent ease by which others have seemed to move past the loss of my daughter. I have sensed from others that I have perhaps grieved too long, or continue feeling things I should not, according to an arbitrary social standard for bereavement. While I have, at times, felt almost a heartlessness from others, one of my greatest comforts has come from the few who not only comprehend the depth of this tragedy, but also share in my grief. The point is that, though the vast majority understand very little about stillbirth, there are some in life who serve as small reminders of true compassion, a willingness to share our immense burden.

My faith, and my wife's faith, in God has also been a tremendously unfailing source of stability in a very uncertain few years. We have many verses and hymns that have sustained us when feeling the most distraught. If there is one thing to know immediately following the loss of a child, it is that very few will truly know the reality of your situation. Knowing that from the outset, or sometime within the first few weeks, might make it a little easier when you experiencing some of the well-intentioned, but ultimately poorly-placed words of those that cannot or will not reach for you when you feel lost, alone, or fragmented from the departure of such a precious, treasured baby.

LT Mark Stanfield, USN

Though the vast majority understand very little about stillbirth, there are some in life who serve as small reminders of true compassion, a willingness to share our immense burden.

SOPHIE

On the 21/06/11 my wife, Jennifer, and I received the devastating news that our first child Sophie-Catherine Mills had passed away whilst still in the womb. We were told we would need to prepare ourselves for Sophie to be delivered naturally as surgery would carry irreversible risks to Jennifer.

Sophie was born two days later with myself and a midwife present. A day that should have been the happiest of Jennifer and I's life was the most painful. We got through each day after Sophie was born; taking one minute of each day at a time. I very quickly went into a mode of making sure that arrangements for Sophie's funeral were taken care of and that Jennifer was okay. After Sophie's funeral, I quickly spiralled into a state of depression and escaped my struggling emotions by drinking a lot of alcohol and feeling so low about myself that I had planned on ending my life and knowing exactly how I would do it. Surely Sophie, Jennifer, my friends and family wouldn't want to see me like this right? But I felt I couldn't cope any other way.

Jen and I regularly met with a bereavement counsellor called Daryl; who was incredible and to this day who we have a close relationship with. She suggested that I needed extended periods of counselling and that Jennifer was coping with the loss of Sophie in a different way than I was. Throughout my private counselling sessions with Daryl; we explored the reasons behind my overwhelming emotions and what I could do to make Sophie's passing into something more positive. "How was this going to be possible?" I thought.

I remember sitting and watching television in our then flat at the edge of the city of Dundee, Scotland and like an epiphany it came to me that we should set up a charity in Sophie's name to help other families affected by the loss of a baby. Jennifer looked up at me with a face that looked at me suggesting I was mad. I think in a way I was, but nonetheless very focused on the idea. We were keen to carry on a legacy for Sophie that would live forever.

Jennifer and I had daily contact with Dr. Pauline Lynch who cared for Jennifer and I whilst Jennifer was in hospital. She also became a person who we had a very close relationship with, although at this point we didn't understand how close.

Dr Lynch, or as we eventually just called her, Pauline, sat us down in her office and suggested we booked a holiday.

"Somewhere far away, warm and sunny," she said. I sat there thinking she was so insensitive. I asked her "How could we just go on holiday after what we had been through?" She smiled and said that she appreciated this was a difficult idea but that going away to unwind would help us to grieve and reconnect as a couple. Jennifer and I for a few days after discussed where we would go. We spoke to her parents, Dave and Joyce, and decided as a family that the four of us would go away together. Greece was where we were going to go. The holiday was fun and, as Dr Lynch suggested, it allowed us to grieve and to reconnect.

In the end, the holiday was very good, but I knew that when we arrived back home that we would set in motion our charity ideas. We made sure not to rush our charity ideas as this was to be something we needed to be sure about and an idea that worked.

Fortunately, Jennifer and I were able to pay for Sophie's funeral and headstone but we got to thinking, "Were other parents of babies able to do this?" We carried out extensive research; both in our geographical area and in the United Kingdom and we identified a need for baby memorials. At that point we knew that we wanted to set up a charity that would aim to raise money to provide lasting memorials to bereaved parents of babies lost through stillbirth or who had died in the first 28 days of life in Tayside, Scotland. We set out with our close friend Rev. Gordon Campbell to complete a large amount of paperwork for the Scottish Charity Regulators to consider giving us charitable status in Scotland. We completed the paperwork and then waited until January 2014 to hear if we had been successful. In January, the charity regulators emailed me with acceptance to have charitable status...FANTASTIC!

We then needed a group of people to recruit who we knew had specific skills. (i.e. accountancy, a spiritual care giver and charity experts.) We recruited a mixture of family and friends. Now came the most complex part - approaching our local hospital and asking our National Health Service whether this is an idea that we could work with them on. Initially they were sceptical, but we managed to talk them into presenting our idea to the head of our local health board. After two meetings with a representative there on our behalf, our proposal to work with the National Health Service was accepted.

We then set to work organising fundraising events, which were very successful and ranged from 25 mile cycles, quizzes, and most recently climbing to the summit of Mount Kilimanjaro in Africa. Our charity has also received private donations, funding from a council in Tayside, funding from a building society, and funding from a major vehicle dealership.

At the time of writing this article, we have assisted to provide 9 memorials and have recruited several new board members - who now includes two surrogate parents, a media expert, an Information Technology expert, Jennifer's doctor, Dr Pauline Lynch, and soon we are to be welcoming a teacher to our board.

We have also identified the need to expand the work that we do and are currently presenting to the Scottish Charity Regulators for our charity to assist more bereaved parents with memorials for their babies and are aiming to assist parents of babies lost through early miscarriage (12 weeks gestation) up until 1 year old.

Jennifer and I are so very proud of what we have achieved and as a few parents and medical experts have said to us, we have turned such a heart breaking tragedy into something so positive. We miss Sophie every day, but are comforted in the fact that she will be looking down on us and knowing what we have down in her memory. We hope she is proud!

Paul Mills

Jennifer and I are so very proud of what we have achieved and as a few parents and medical experts have said to us, we have turned such a heart breaking tragedy into something so positive. We miss Sophie every day, but are comforted in the fact that she will be looking down on us and knowing what we have down in her memory. We hope she is proud!

SAM. LEAH. PHOEBE. HARRIET.

"I'm so sorry... there's no heartbeat."

Six little words that I thought I couldn't possibly hear AGAIN, could I?

Again, because this wasn't our first time around.
Again, because this wasn't our first loss.
Again, because this wasn't our first encounter with having hope, dreams and longings... dashed on the rocks, snatched away, ripped out from under us.

Our first experience of baby loss was after 12 weeks of pregnancy.
12 weeks of excitedly keeping up-to-date with how our little one was developing and growing on a daily basis.
12 weeks of telling all of our family and friends our big, life-changing news.
12 weeks of making plans like nursery decorations, colour schemes, tiny clothes and pushchair-shopping.

How naïve were we?!

Nothing can prepare you for having to have those painful conversations with family members and friends... feeling like we're somehow letting them down... the bearers of such bad news... of seeing my Mom crumpled and crushed under the grief of hearing me telling her that she's not going to be a 'Nanny.'

Within all the hurt and emotions and feelings, how messed up am I, that one of the worst things I felt like I was going through, was that we were letting SO many other people down with our bad news?!

Since hearing those six words the first time, where we found out that we had lost our baby boy at 12 weeks, we have had to endure the same loss twice more.

And even though, each time, the story ended the same way, the experiences and emotions were fresh, different and painful in new (and unwanted) ways.

After losing our baby boy, we were put on the 'at risk' list. Not a list that I would wish anyone to be put on.
The assumption (that it feels like is being made about us as a couple) is that we are somehow inferior... like there's something that we have done (or haven't done) to mean that

we have been put on this list… we're the ones to blame… we're the problem to be 'solved' or the issue to be 'put up with.'

Our following pregnancy (eventually coming 2 years after our first loss AND culminating in the successful pregnancy and birth of our daughter) was fraught with dread, suspicion, hesitation and tentativeness.

Would today be the day?

The day my wife couldn't feel any movement?

The day the horrendous (and inevitable) happened to us again?

The day we received the bad news from the midwife, doctor or sonographer?

The day we heard those 'six words' again?

This time around we limited who and what we told about our news.

This time around there were no shopping trips to mothercare…

This time around there were no colour schemes or nursery furniture plans or looking forward at all.

That sinking feeling and the horrible waiting for bad-news would be the shadow that was cast over the entire pregnancy.

I tried my best to stay positive and strong for my pregnant

wife, who (I felt) was relying on me to be the strong supportive spouse... but underneath, the whole time, I was terrified.

Even after the birth of our daughter, I was STILL waiting for there to be some kind of incurable birth-defect or complications at the hospital... and the fear didn't end there... countless nights of expecting cot-death or to come home to a devastated wife who would tell me that our little girl hadn't made it through the day.

It is only with hindsight, that I can recognise that our experience with our first pregnancy had robbed us of the 'normal' joy of the pregnancy/birth experience of our daughter.
All those months of counting down, anticipating, midwife check-ups and baby scans that SHOULD have been a wonderfully blessed time of our lives, we're ACTUALLY some of the most terrifying and stressful times.

And I wish that I could say that THAT was the end of the story... that we'd been through hell-and-back once and then we got the child we were longing for and we all lived happily ever after... but I can't.
Because that's not how the story goes.
Because that's not how life goes.

Since having our daughter, we have lost two more babies.
Both little girls.
Both in the third trimester of pregnancy.
Both times hearing those six soul-destroying words.

"I'm so sorry, there's no heartbeat."

So, that's our lot.
Two miscarriages and one medically-induced still-birth.

As a husband, as a father, this has been a slow and silent kind of torture.
As a Christian and church attender (and Pastor of a church)... I wish that I could say that I could make some kind of divine-sense of what we went through.

Church family and friends offered bible verses and platitudes (that I'm sure they thought would help)... things like, "God works in mysterious ways" and "It's all part of the Lord's plan" and "Ours is not to question" and "God only gives us things that we can handle"... and they meant well.

They were trying to help.
They were trying to be a comfort.
They felt like they needed to say something.

But, the truth is, they didn't.

Help was the last thing we needed.
Comfort was never going to come through words.
We really didn't need the silence filled.

All we wanted... all I wanted was for it to be acknowledged.
That this was shit.
That it was ok to be angry.
That it was natural to have questions.

When all I wanted and needed was people to be WITH me,
to sit IN this, to allow me the time and space to just BE...
that was the last thing anyone was willing to offer.

As a husband, I felt helpless.
All I could do was stand by and watch as my bubbly, out-
going, fun-loving and life-filled wife crumpled into nothing.
An empty shell.
All dried up with no tears left to cry.
Shut away in the dark, refusing to leave the house, refusing
to see or speak to anyone.

As a husband, I was SUPPOSED to be the strong one.
I was supposed to support, defend, protect and provide for
my family...
But all I felt like was a total failure.

My one job... my only role... and I couldn't.

And there was no one to talk to.

Nobody to share my feelings and experiences with.

Church was supposed to be family.

Church was supposed to be my support network.

A home away from home.

But instead, all church became was a place FULL of people where I felt even more alone.

I didn't think there could be anything worse than those times spent in scan rooms, hearing those six words, looking down into the lost and helpless eyes of my, once so joyful, wife...

I didn't think there could be anything worse than seeing the tiny white coffin and performing the funeral service for your own unborn child to a crowd of two (my grieving wife and a funeral director)...

I didn't think there could be anything worse that having to wait to see our grievance counsellor, sat in the waiting room of a women's hospital, the whole time being passed by women in various stages of pregnancy.

I didn't think there could be anything worse than experiencing the awkward silences, the down-turned, pitying looks and all the times NOT being invited out to things by people who were supposed to be friends and family.

But I was wrong.
It's all the everyday stuff.
The constant reminders.
The normal things like, birthday parties and day-trips.
The realisation that I can't remember the last time I cried for my babies.
The sinking feeling that I can't remember the last time that I thought about them... and yet...

And yet, I think about them ALL the time.

And yet, there's a beauty within this brokenness.

And yet, there's grace in even times like this.

And yet, the shadows still manage to prove that the sun DOES shine.

And yet, I wouldn't be where I am today without that messed-up bunch of people I call "family."

And yet, I wouldn't be who I am today without my wounds and scars.

And yet, grace has a way of showing up in the most

unexpected ways.

And yet, love has a way of revealing itself in the most unusual times.

So, with a heavy heart and with tears in my eyes, I speak my children's names.

Sam. Leah. Phoebe. Harriet.

Stephen Parkes

They were trying to help.

They were trying to be a comfort.
They felt like they needed to say something.
But, the truth is, they didn't.
Help was the last thing we needed.
Comfort was never going to come through words.
We really didn't need the silence filled.

All we wanted… all I wanted was for it to be
acknowledged.
That this was shit.
That it was ok to be angry.
That it was natural to have questions.
When all I wanted and needed was people to be
WITH me, to sit IN this, to allow me the time and
space to just BE… that was the last thing anyone
was willing to offer.

ASHER RAY

A common theme that I am sure will resonate throughout the submissions to this book is the stereotype that surrounds men and their grief. The world in which we live paints a picture of what a man should feel and the emotions that he should or should not exude throughout his life. Unfortunately, this stereotype forces men to become emotionless robots who train themselves to bury their feelings at an early age. Whether this ideal is bestowed upon these men via their parents, media, books, etc., it is one that persists throughout the generations. It is also one that I myself adopted and attempted to maintain throughout my entire life. This ideal was only truly challenged the day that I held my stillborn son.

Like many other people, I have always planned out my life in a series of stages: graduate high school, get into college, graduate college, get a job, get married, buy a house, have a kid. I have always found myself checking each of these boxes with ease and have felt blessed to be able to find the love of my life, get a great job, and purchase my own house before the age of 26. It was not until I arrived at the final check box that I truly struggled. My wife and I did not effortlessly check off that final box and found ourselves walking down a path of fertility treatments, a miscarriage, a D&C, and continued failed treatments. Then, finally, we were blessed with a positive pregnancy test after we thought all was lost. I felt like I could finally check off that final box and live the fairytale life that I always envisioned for myself. Just as I readied the pen to solidify that final stage devastation struck. On February 18th, 2017 my beautiful son no longer had a heartbeat and on February 19th, 2017 my son was born still.

The moment that the ultrasound tech desperately tried to find a non-existent heartbeat and the doctor that was present slowly shook her head to indicate that my son had passed is one that will be engrained in my head for the rest of my life. It was in that moment that all the years of repressing my feelings and "acting like a man" were thrown out the window and I became consumed by grief. While I have experienced sadness through the loss of loved ones and difficult moments in my life before nothing will ever compare to the tears that were shed for my son. All I could do was hold my wife and shed every tear my body could. It almost felt like a dream and I felt myself asking questions like why did this happen to me and what did we do wrong? Before I knew it, we were calling our family members to inform them of the news and being taken back to a room to await the next stage. Unfortunately, this stage was my wife having to give birth to our son.

Before I knew it, I found myself reverting back into the strong husband to be the rock that my wife needed through the next 24 hours. The strength my wife showed leading up to and after my son's birth is one that no person in the world could ever match. After being induced, our beautiful boy was born at 2:18pm. Once again, I reverted out of my personalized shell and shed tears as I held my son in my arms. He was the most beautiful thing that I had ever seen but I could not take him home with me and this feeling became more and more evident as his skin color changed. We took pictures and I did my best to try and not portray a look of defeat on my face but I could not. I felt like I had failed not only because I lost my son but also because I could not bottle up those feelings and be the man I had been my entire life. This is probably the most unfortunate thing because no man should be ashamed for showing his emotions, especially in such a moment as this.

The days after my son's death felt like years. My wife and I felt guilty attempting to do anything to entertain ourselves so our hours were spent trying to do things for our son like baking cookies for our amazing nurses, making a shadow box for him, and doing whatever we could in his memory. The largest hurdle for me during this grief process was going into our son's room. We had spent so much time preparing it for his arrival and now it would not be filled with love and noises of babies crying. After days of sulking, commemorating our son in any way we could think of, and lots of puzzles (the only thing we could do to keep busy that didn't make us feel extremely guilty), we finally entered our little boy's room. What I thought would be a moment of immense sadness actually became one of relief. I was definitely saddened by the sight of his empty crib and all the things we had gotten ready for him, I also felt as if I could be closer to him in his room and that we finally had a place to put his ashes and see him whenever we wanted. His room has remained open ever since.

After a few weeks, I went back to work. This was a day that I was dreading because it not only meant leaving my wife at home but it also meant facing my colleagues at work and being given the same rote message of "I am so sorry for your loss." I actually quarantined myself to avoid this because I still wanted to maintain that emotionless persona that felt so comfortable. I made it through my first day, then my first week, and before I knew it, it had been a month since my beautiful boy passed away. It was then that people stopped asking how I was and attempted to return to normal. Where

I first avoided people's sympathy, I then found myself angry at them for no longer asking. My reality was that every day I woke up knowing that I had lost my son, but this is something my colleagues could not comprehend and tried to avoid thinking about. They would occasionally ask how my wife and I were doing but it felt so forced and uncaring. This is when I came to the realization that while others would move on from recognizing my loss, I would live with it for the rest of my life. Worst of all, this mentality spread to friends and even, in some cases, family. It is at this point my wife and I sought out the loss community which is a decision I am grateful for to this day.

Many people in the loss community will agree that being a part of this "club" is one of the best and worst things. It is the best because the people that belong to this community are some of the most caring and selfless people you will ever meet. However, it is the worst because you are brought together by the loss of a child. It is with this group that I met like-minded people and couples that truly understood my grief. Best of all, I met other men who were experiencing the same emotions and attempting to keep their machismo intact. A character flaw we all share and one that we all wish we did not have. Being able to share my feelings and talk about my grief has been helpful.

It has been over a year since my son's death and I regretfully have reverted back to my old self in many respects. I swallow my emotions, remain strong for my wife when she needs me to be, and keep my sadness at bay. However, even though this notion of needing to bottle up my feelings remains, I still find my emotions peek through every time I think about my son. While this experience is long gone in the minds of friends, of family, it is one that my wife and I live with on a daily basis and will continue to think about until our dying days. I will continue to celebrate my son in any way I can and his memory will remain with me forever.

In loving memory of Asher Ray.

Steven Lied

https://theluckyanchorproject.wordpress.com

I came to the realization that while others would move on from recognizing my loss, I would live with it for the rest of my life. Worst of all, this mentality spread to friends and even, in some cases, family. It is at this point my wife and I sought out the loss community which is a decision I am grateful for to this day.

Many people in the loss community will agree that being a part of this "club" is one of the best and worst things. It is the best because the people that belong to this community are some of the most caring and selfless people you will ever meet. However, it is the worst because you are brought together by the loss of a child. It is with this group that I met like-minded people and couples that truly understood my grief. Best of all, I met other men who were experiencing the same emotions and attempting to keep their machismo intact. A character flaw we all share and one that we all wish we did not have. Being able to share my feelings and talk about my grief has been helpful.

OLIVER

Losing a child is one of the worst things that can happen.
It's not a pity party like most think, it goes against nature
- no parent should ever have to bury their child. It's not
normal and it's impossible for anyone to understand unless
it happens to them.

Now I can only talk from my own experiences of losing our
son, some may have had a similar experience and some may
not, but that's ok. There is no set guide for child loss and no
set way to grieve.

A bit of background on me before our loss - I was outgoing,
quite bubbly, quite a positive person, and took pride in my
appearance.

Oliver was born close to 27 weeks. His mother had nearly
died due to pre-eclampsia the night before. He was with
us and fighting for 19 hours, we sat there watching them
work on him due to a hemorrhage. The pain of having to
sit there watching your son die is something I can't even
begin to describe. Oliver's mother had to be drugged up and
brought around as she was quite ill. The look on her face is

one I never want to have to witness again and I assumed the typical male role of reassuring her, telling her everything would be OK and being strong.

As we left the room with him in a Moses basket and her in front of me, I broke down and sobbed like I've never sobbed before to the point that I nearly collapsed. I quickly composed myself and we were taken to a private room where we did the typical things, like calling the family. Again, this is not something I ever want to do again.

The day after, we were given a memory box. I can't even begin to describe what this meant to me and Nicole, the memory box was from a charity called 4Louis. In it was a clay kit for making footprints and handprints and other various items which brought great comfort. Please check them out at http://www.4louis.co.uk/

Over the next few days family and some very close friends came to visit, to see Oliver and hold him. I can't even express in words how much this meant to myself and Nicole - the one picture that stands out to me still is one of my parents. The heartbreak the picture shows still make me very sad every time is see it.

Fast forward a few weeks when we finally left the hospital. Life just felt pointless and empty and we both struggled massively. Because Nicole had been very ill, I once again took to the typical male role of being strong for her. After a few months as Nicole became physically stronger health wise, I crashed like a ton of bricks.

The only support at this point I was offered was tablets. I had tried to speak with SANDS to be told there was nothing available to men in my area. At that point, I took the tablets and stopped looking for help. The tablets helped with the extreme anxiety attacks I was getting and the depression, but eventually I stopped taking them as they had made me feel emotionless and I didn't like that.

In December of that year something changed and I began to pull myself out. Of course, the support we got from family and from each other contributed to this, but as most men can be, I am typically stubborn and don't discuss things very often. As is most often is the case, I ignored most people who were doing their best to offer support. The next few months were up and down, I started working again which gave me a new purpose, but still it felt like we were just existing there wasn't much joy.

In 2014, we found out we were expecting our rainbow baby.

Everything that had started to level out hit an all-time low again. You see, once you lose a child pregnancy is no longer the joyous occasion it should be. People reading this might think that's a ungrateful and negative view but it's the honest truth.

The general understanding by non-angel parents is having another child will fix things. This simply is not true and I can't even describe how much pain that causes hearing those very words. Now, you know all too well that you might not get to bring your baby home, so how could you be happy? Not to mention all the emotions it brings back and the terrifying feeling of fear for "What if it happens again?"

The entire pregnancy of our rainbow was a traumatic experience, with the preeclampsia rearing it head again. Thankfully she was closely monitored this time and kept in for the last 6 weeks of the pregnancy - this in itself added more emotions on top of the ones we already were feeling.

On September the 23rd, we welcomed our precious rainbow into the world. A healthy baby girl, for the next few weeks things were better, or so I thought. A busy mind is a distracted mind and as things settled down the feeling of emptiness returned and the low moods came again. Again I did the typical man thing and stayed strong as my partner was struggling with her emotions, as a side effect of the c section and epidural. My partner was left with unrepairable nerve damage on her back adding even more stress on top of our daily struggles.

As I sit here today typing this , I realize how much I have changed, for the most part for the better - being able to give back through making graphics for people and volunteering for Daddy's With Angels. I am also slightly more irritable than before my loss and have anger problems that I am working on.

Daddy's With Angels is unique in that it is ran by men for men. Roughly a year after joining, I was asked if I would like to volunteer my time and haven't looked back since.

Warren Morris

My blog site is https://oliversdaddy.co.uk

www.daddyswithangels.org - offering online peer to peer support groups

The only support at this point I was offered was tablets. I had tried to speak with SANDS to be told there was nothing available to men in my area. At that point, I took the tablets and stopped looking for help. The tablets helped with the extreme anxiety attacks I was getting and the depression, but eventually I stopped taking them as they had made me feel emotionless and I didn't like that.

ELIJAH

My only son was stillborn in November of 2014. We had been told at the ultrasound visits that his heart was not that strong. We were positive people so, obviously, there were things bought. However, also being realistic, there were conversations had. One of them was about organ donation. We had easily decided to donate his organs if he didn't make it. We had decided, if we would be willing to accept a heart if he needs one, there is no reason to deny anyone else that may need something if he doesn't.

The evening he was born we were so not prepared. No matter how many doctors say, no matter how many weeks you have, you are not prepared. You hear so many people talking about beautiful babies, and they are. Your life, combined with another life, to create life. This beautiful child, has my hands, yet no life. What has happened? I blamed myself. "Was it my fault?" "Could I have done something different?" "Was it genetic?" This is the darkest place a person can be.

Fortunately, for me, I was working at a psychiatric hospital at the time. Because I was afraid of the outcome, I never let my co-workers know that I was expecting. When the two that did know finally got ahold of me and heard the news, they asked to talk. They gave me names of support groups I would have never known about as nobody expects this. Talking with people does help. And you do, sometimes you do, alienate everyone that has no idea what you are going through. I did. She had two other kids that she was trying to get to understand the loss. I couldn't relate.

I had just lost my only child. When there is no explanation for you, you can't give one to someone else. You can't even try. They know why you disappear on his birthday. Four years and it's still hard to explain why I disappear on mine, four days before Father's Day.

Fortunately, I have met some new friends. They don't know me from before and are willing to "get my bits," and understand my strength. I talk about him, to make him feel here. My family knows my loss, as do people in other groups. It is a sadness that we will carry forever. Talking about it helps. Please do, and reach out.
Say your child's name.

My favorite thing is someone acknowledging that he was here.

William Colburn

Helpful sites:

https://missfoundation.org

www.irisremembers.com

The evening he was born we were so not prepared. No matter how many doctors say, no matter how many weeks you have, you are not prepared. You hear so many people talking about beautiful babies, and they are. Your life, combined with another life, to create life. This beautiful child, has my hands, yet no life. What has happened?

MICHAEL JOSEPH (MJ)

What happens when your faith in this life is put to the test? There have been many challenges and tests along my path through life. None, however, more than when my son Michael Joseph, who we called MJ, was in the hospital fighting for his life for 35 days and then when he passed away. To say that my religious faith was and is still tested is an understatement. Like rolling prairie hills during fire season, each hill comes with either calm green prairie grass, or raging red flames or anger, consuming my faith and reducing it to ash.

Throughout my life my faith has always been tested. From sports, to school, to church, faith was a common theme woven in the challenges faced. Growing up in California and attending a Baptist church most Sundays and vacation bible school in the summers, I would make the argument that I have a good foundation of faith. As I grew older faith and religion became something very personal and away from the organized religion of the church. I found organized religion to be to entangled with politics that pushed me to take religion individually.

My wife and I found out early in her pregnancy that we were having twin boys. After battles with infertility, this news was a blessing and my faith became stronger than before because I prayed that we would be blessed to start a family. So eager to see my twins, even for just a glimpse, I eagerly awaited the 20-week ultrasound. Often this ultrasound is called the gender ultrasound for the parents, family, and friends, but medically it is a critical anatomy scan. On that day my world changed forever and my faith has never been the same.

When the doctor broke the news to me and my wife, he looked at us and told us we needed to decide right then and there if we would remain married or be a divorce statistic. My faith would be tested and the conversation with my wife would lead to us putting 100% effort and support into each other no matter what. At this point my faith remained strong because we never thought that anything bad would happen and both our boys would come home from the hospital. My faith reminded strong throughout the pregnancy as the weight of mountains were on our shoulders with countless ultrasounds, an excruciating fetal MRI for my wife, countless specialist doctor visits, and through the fog of statistics associated with MJ's diagnosis of a Congenital Diaphragmatic Hernia.

The day my boys were born was the day my faith was shaken but not gone - small cracks on the surface of my faith. The realization of my son being born blue, not breathing or having the capacity to breath on his own, and the several doctors whisking him away to allow him a chance to live. It was a traumatic birth of my boys who were eventually born via C-section after 24 hours of labor, 2 hours of pushing, one request for the C-Section, and a pissed off nurse who slammed her fists on my wife's hospital bed as if she just lost a bet. My wife began hemorrhaging after the birth and I was rushed away from her bed side not knowing if she would live or not, and thinking my last vision of my wife would be that of a nurse (who slammed her fists on her bed before my children were born) on top of my wife pushing with all her might and screaming for me to leave. Needless to say, my faith became more cracked and pieces of my faith were beginning to remain on the hospital floor.

It was not until almost 24 hours later when my wife could see MJ with me. Restoring my faith through prayers that she would be healthy enough to see MJ that night made me realize that not all prayers were unanswered. My wife and I were able to see our son MJ that night briefly to say hello and tell him we loved him. The first sight of so many machines and the realization that his medical condition was very serious. Throughout my wife's pregnancy we shielded ourselves from reality, statistics, and the scenario that would be our reality.

Doctors told us not to long after this, that if MJ made it through the night we would be lucky. Still numb with the reality of how sick MJ was, we still did not think he would die. Still living and breathing on prayers and hope, we prayed MJ would make it through the night and could not believe how dramatic the doctor was being because we were still blinded by the belief that our baby would not die. MJ did make it through the night and would need to be transferred to a different hospital due to needing a machine called ECMO. In our research before birth, ECMO was extremely scary and the reality of our son's inevitable death fell on me as a pile of boulders. With this new information and weight on the world fell upon our shoulders as first-time parents, now with a critically ill son.

When MJ was transferred to the second hospital and my wife was discharged, MJ was put on ECMO and the roller coaster of emotions, faith, prayer, thoughts, and trauma began. During the hospital stay at the second hospital there was countless events that challenged my faith and religious beliefs. None more than after MJ's CDH repair surgery. With the amount of trauma on his tiny body through this surgery his organs began to shut down. MJ's body was retaining all fluids and this was the first time in my life I prayed for someone to pee. I prayed non-stop, wondering how much fluid a little boy could hold. I remember him being so sick and me praying for pee. I remember the moment my prayers were answered and his pee began to flow, I felt a real relief and that we were now on the way to MJ becoming stable.

For a few days MJ began to improve and I felt a close relationship with faith and god that I have not felt since I was baptized. I grew up in a Baptist church and was baptized and saved at an age where I had to justify and rationalize (to the best I could at the approximate age of 9 years old). I attended a religious college (Catholic) on a sports scholarship and that is where I met my wife and life-long friends. With the religious aspect of college, but not a practicing Catholic, I had religious conversations with friends and my faith grew. Although I would have to say that my faith grew but my desire to attend an organized religious establishment disintegrated.

On my wife's birthday my son was extremely sick and the doctors told us we needed to be there. I reached into my soul to pray to god that our son would not die on my wife's birthday, forever impacting her birthday to the fullest. Looking back, I guess that this prayer being answered was like a consolation prize for a lifetime of grief. That night I then began to pray somehow, someway, that god would heal MJ completely and take my soul instead. I prayed time and time again throughout MJ's 35 days of life to trade places and he live and I die but none as powerful as that night. I wanted my wife to have both of our boys in her arms and not one in her arms and one in her heart, even if that meant she would not have me.

The evening after my wife's birthday our son MJ died in our arms surrounded by family, friends, and the most outstanding doctors and nurses we could ask for. I remember being numb to my very soul because I felt that my son would never die. Angry with god, religion, and faith I did not know what to do but fake it until I could make it.

My faith has been shaken and pushed off the path. Today I feel like I have to believe in god, heaven, faith, the soul, and religion because if I do not then that simply means I will not see my son MJ again, or that he is not in heaven, or that his soul does not exist. I question my religion each and every day with mixed conclusions, like a maze with countless paths and exits. Creating a new scenario, conclusion, and belief each and every day. In a world where healthy and sick babies are born every day I struggle with the thought that so many babies are critical ill or disabled. Why would god give people critically ill babies? Why do we get to love a child for a short time? I do not have answers to these earthly questions but I hope to be able to ask them one day.

My faith and relationship with god has been rocked to the core. My foundational beliefs challenged, and my understanding of the world, afterlife, and heaven have been heavily altered. I hope I can begin to regain my relationship with god and come to an earthly understanding until I can contemplate these circumstances and grasp the understanding without the constraints of the human brain. I struggled to writing this because to grasp the understanding of my faith and relationship with god means I have to have some concrete understanding of my faith. My faith and relationship seem to shift with the wind, as does my relationship with the lord.

William Skaggs

My faith has been shaken and pushed off the path. Today I feel like I have to believe in god, heaven, faith, the soul, and religion because if I do not then that simply means I will not see my son MJ again, or that he is not in heaven, or that his soul does not exist. I question my religion each and every day with mixed conclusions, like a maze with countless paths and exits. Creating a new scenario, conclusion, and belief each and every day.

LILLIAN RAE

There was no warning for me. One moment I was working my station at the hospital, the next my wife was there telling me she was going up to the triage. My heart instantly sank, my wife who works in maternity, knew that something was not right. She assured me that all was ok and to keep working, but I was not going to let her go alone. I simply went and clocked out and went with her. This was just the start of the worst day of my life. It was not long after getting to triage that we found out that we had lost our baby, Lilly, at almost eighteen weeks. My heart that had been filled with such joy had now been shattered into a million pieces. To this day it has not recovered and most likely will not ever recover from losing her. It was not supposed to happen to us. You hear of it all the time, but it is not something that you ever expect to happen to you. But yet there we were with loved ones around, awaiting the arrival of our precious baby girl that we would not get to see grow up. All of the hopes and dreams we had for her were taken away.

We had a small graveside service for our baby girl, but it all just seems like a blur to me. I remember thinking that

I wanted to carry her little casket to where she would be buried, though when I arrived they had already placed it at where she would be buried. Looking back, I believe that was probably for the best. After everything was done, all my wife and I knew was that we had to get away from everyone and everything. We took off on a trip for the sole purpose of we didn't want to see anyone that we knew or talk about our loss. We did our best to avoid people that would try to console us, because to us there was no consoling that could help. Once there, we realized that trying to escape did us no good. We couldn't escape it and we needed support. Though it felt like there was only enough support for her most of the time.

Unfortunately for me, I was Dad. So what that meant was I was only allowed to be away from work for just a few days before I had to start using vacation time to be away as well as having the concern of absence counting against me. So around a week after losing my precious little girl, I was back at work. No one knew what to say to me, some just avoided me it felt like. But it seemed like whenever someone finally did decide to talk to me, it was always about Lilly's mommy. Please do not get me wrong, I did not take offense to them asking about her, it was just after asking about her that was it. Most people would not bother to ask how I was doing, I felt forgotten during all of this.

I was getting told to be strong for her and inside of my head I was screaming at the top of my lungs, "What about me!" But that is the other curse of being a loss father, it almost feels as if it is expected that you must not show emotion to your significant other because you are supposed to be the strong one. The one thing that I was thankful for was my wife's co-workers. Because other than my immediate family, they understood better than almost anyone that I had lost my baby as well. Each day they saw me they made sure to check on me first, then would proceed to ask how my wife was doing. They got it. Though that was most likely because many of them were there during that moment and understood the love that I had for my little girl as well.

If there was one thing that I would have changed during this, it would have been how I responded to all of the people who would simply ask how Mom was doing. I believe that maybe if I had handled my responses to them better, then maybe those individuals would have understood how much I was hurting as well. Possibly then I would have had a few more shoulders just to lean on and been able to say, "I'm having a bad day" instead of isolating myself at work and just getting through it by myself. I have found though, contrary to popular belief, time does not heal all wounds.

Zach Storer

I have found though, contrary to popular belief, time does not heal all wounds.

Online Resources for Support

at the time of publication

- www.emilyrlong.com

- www.AFatherOfLoss.com

- Essay "To Grieve": http://www.performan-cephilosophy.org/journal/article/view/10/27

- https://www.facebook.com/mjsmemories/

- www.stillstandingmag.com

- https://www.facebook.com/GrievingDads/

- https://www.facebook.com/groups/Grieving-fathers/

- http://maya.stephenson.muchloved.com

- geekycatholicdad.blogspot.com

- "Too Wonderful (Asher's Song)" https://www.youtube.com/watch?v=xnLcTc0rUzg

- http://www.facebook.com/mannysfund

- www.lostlullabies.weebly.com

- www.ourangelscharity.co.uk

- https://missfoundation.org

- www.irisremembers.com

- www.thetearsfoundation.org/newhampshire

- Dad's of Steele

- https://theluckyanchorproject.wordpress.com/

- https://oliversdaddy.co.uk

- www.daddyswithangels.org - offering online peer to peer support groups

Other Available Books by Emily:

- Invisible Mothers: When Love Doesn't Die (September 2015)

- You Are Not Alone: Love Letters from Loss Mom to Loss Mom (April 2016)

- From Father to Father: Letters from Loss Dad to Loss Dad (November 2016)

- Life Without the Baby Journal: Redefining Life, Motherhood and Self After Loss (March 2017)

- From Mother to Mother: On the Loss of a Child (September 2017)